"If you don't make the time to work on creating the life you want, you're eventually going to be forced to spend a LOT of time dealing with a life you don't want."

KEVIN NGO

"It's how we spend our time here and now, that really matters. If you are fed up with the way you have come to interact with time, change it."

MARCIA WEIDER

Other Resources by Lee Cockerell

BOOKS
Creating Magic
10 Common Sense Leadership Strategies from a Life at Disney

The Customer Rules
The 39 Essential Rules for Delivering Sensational Service

Career Magic
How to Stay on Track to Achieve a Stellar Career

SMARTPHONE APPS
Creating Magic—Leadership & Coaching on the Go!
iPhone App

TEACHER'S GUIDES
**Teacher's Guide for Creating Magic
and Time Management Magic**
Go to *www.LeeCockerell.com* to download and print

WEBSITES
www.LeeCockerell.com
*Weekly leadership thoughts, seminars,
keynote speeches, blog & podcast*

www.Thrive15.com
*15-minute videos to move your life and career from
surviving to thriving (Free to veterans)*

www.TheSportsMindInstitute.com
*The Life Lessons of Sports—Extraordinary people
who share personal stories about their relationship
with sports well beyond the scoreboard*

PODCAST (15 minutes weekly)
Creating Disney Magic Podcast on iTunes, iHeart Radio,
Stitcher Radio and on my website www.LeeCockerell.com

TIME
MANAGEMENT
MAGIC

How To Get More Done Every Day
Move From Surviving To Thriving

Lee Cockerell

emerge
publishing

TULSA, OKLAHOMA

TULSA, OKLAHOMA

Published by:
Emerge Publishing, llc
9521B Riverside Parkway Suite #243
Tulsa, Oklahoma 74137
Phone: (888) 407-4447
Visit our web site at *www.EmergePublishing.com*

Library of Congress Cataloging-in-Publication Data
Cockerell, Lee
Time management magic: how to get more done every day
move from surviving to thriving / by Lee Cockerell.

ISBN: 978-1-943127-31-3 (paperback)
ISBN: 978-0-9907694-6-0 (hardback)
ISBN: 978-0-9907694-3-9 (e-book)

BUS088000
BUSINESS & ECONOMICS / Time Management

Cover and interior design: Christian Ophus/Emerge Publishing, llc.

Printed in the United States of America.

This book is dedicated to my grandmother,

Jo Ella Pomeroy Cook, who gave me my first watch

on my fifth birthday and always had time for me.

"The day is of infinite length for him who knows how to appreciate and use it."

JOHANN WOLFGANG VON GOETHE

TABLE OF CONTENTS

"I'm definitely going to take a course on time management... just as soon as I can work it into my schedule."

LOUIS E. BOONE

FOREWORD

Some people make their dreams come true by meticulously charting their route and following their plan without deviating. Other people reach their potential by greeting each new day, recognizing it as an opportunity, seeing where it leads and going where their instincts direct. Lee Cockerell is one such man. He is a world-renowned speaker, a best-selling author and the retired Executive Vice President of Operations for *Walt Disney World® Resort*, a position he held for ten years. Before working with Disney for sixteen years in Paris and Orlando, Lee worked for Hilton Hotels for eight years and Marriott International for seventeen years.

His books, **Creating Magic** and **The Customer Rules** have inspired countless people around the world to understand how they can create their own magic and deliver world-class customer service.

Lee Cockerell's success is truly "self-made." Becoming a success was neither easy or quick, nor was it planned. He began life on a farm in Oklahoma. His family had no money or indoor plumbing. One of his first jobs was at the age of 8. He had to milk a cow by hand and sell the milk to neighbors. He was expected to do this every day. Since the cow didn't have a day off, neither did Lee.

In hindsight, this job had far-reaching ramifications. It taught him responsibility, accountability and laid the groundwork for the personal discipline that became part of the very fabric of his life.

Time Management Magic is all about learning a system and a way of thinking which will enhance your ability to lead a highly productive, balanced and effective life.

Lee dropped out of college after two years and joined the army in 1964.

Why did Lee succeed where many others failed after dropping out of college and living without a "master plan?" He believes it was his ability to be highly organized, disciplined and to have a positive can-do attitude.

Lee's advice to everyone is, *"Don't underestimate what you can achieve."* *Too many people get discouraged and want to quit because they have setbacks, but that is precisely when you shouldn't quit. Think about this: Why quit when success could be waiting for you just around the next corner? It's not going to get better if you quit. Life is all about your attitude. You are the author of your own story. You create your own magic. The greatest job is the job you have. Give it your all, be the best at what you do and never stop learning. If you do this, when the next opportunity comes, you will be ready for it.*" Getting organized is the key to preparing yourself.

Lee is now retired from Disney but he hasn't retired from making a positive difference in the world. He travels extensively, speaking at seminars and giving keynote speeches about how to become a better leader, a better manager and how to achieve world-class customer service.

Enjoy *Time Management Magic...* It will change your life!

*"Someday, ASAP, and
when I get time... is not a system."*

LEE COCKERELL

INTRODUCTION

It is not *Disney* magic that will make your life work.
It is the way you work that will make your life Magical!

During my time as the Executive Vice President of Operations for the *Walt Disney World®* Resort, I witnessed firsthand how our team created the magical guest experiences, fantastic theme park rides and unique attractions that make *Disney World* the happiest place on Earth. However, even the most talented *Disney Cast Members* have yet to find a way to extend the amount of time you and I have by even one second. Therefore, we still find ourselves running out of time, wishing we had more time, and always feeling like we need just one more second, one more minute, or one more day. It seems that everyone is constantly struggling to manage their time.

During my career at *Disney*, I eventually found myself leading 40,000 Cast Members (employees). I had to become a time management expert, first as a means of survival and then as a way to help others make the best use of their time.

Today, as I travel around the world teaching the leadership principles that I used while I was in the U.S. Army and in my 42-year career at Hilton Hotels, Marriott International and the *Walt Disney Company* in France and Orlando, I am always asked how I managed my time. People wonder how I was able to get anything done while being responsible for the results produced by 40,000 people. So I decided to use some of my time each morning to write down everything I've learned about managing time. My goal is to help others learn these techniques early in life, so they do not make the same mistakes I made before I had a good time management system.

However, this book is not only about Time Management. **It is about Life Management.** "Management" is defined as the act of controlling. This book will help you keep all parts of your life under control.

If, after learning the techniques in the book, you find that you want to learn even more about this concept of Life Management, I highly recommend that you attend a live class. Visit my website, **www.LeeCockerell.com** for information about engaging me to teach this subject to your organization.

I also recommend visiting www.Thrive15.com. Thrive15 provides entertaining and powerful 15-minute education and training videos on this subject and nearly every other subject you and your organization need to become truly successful. Here's another advantage of joining Thrive15. With every paid membership, one *free* membership is given to a veteran of the armed services. This program is called One for One. As a huge supporter of our military, I went to Iraq in 2011 to teach 13 seminars to our warriors and the State Department in the U.S. embassy in Baghdad, I am proud to be associated with this program.

My own website, www.LeeCockerell.com also provides a **"LEADERSHIP THOUGHT FOR THE WEEK"** every Monday morning, plus an archive section with all the past "Leadership Thoughts" and my "Lessons in Leadership" blog. This blog contains over 500 posts on how to be a better leader and a better manager, along with numerous tips on how to vastly improve customer service in your organization.

Also on my personal website there is information about my smartphone app for iPhone and Android, titled *Creating Magic – Leadership & Coaching on the Go* and my books, *Creating Magic, The Customer Rules* and this book, *Time Management Magic*. All these resources give you practical knowledge on how to achieve world-class leadership, management and customer service excellence.

Always remember what I tell my audiences and my family members:

"IT'S NEVER TOO LATE TO GET BETTER!"

The bottom line is, we can all do a better job of implementing time and life management in our daily lives.

This system is like any other system. You can learn to do it just as you can learn other things. Remember that everything is hard before it is easy, but when you master the hard things, life gets easier.

Finally, I have two predictions for you. When you finish reading this book, you will:

1) Believe, without a doubt, that there are many things you can do to manage your life more effectively and efficiently.

2) Be ready to implement an easy system for planning your goals and achieving them.

"Don't say you don't have enough time.
You have exactly the same number of hours
per day that were given to Helen Keller, Pasteur,
Michelangelo, Mother Teresa, Leonardo da Vinci,
Thomas Jefferson, and Albert Einstein."

H. JACKSON BROWN

CHAPTER 1

This Is Your Life!

One of the most important things you can do is to sit down and think deeply about how you spend your time, where you *don't* spend your time and where you *should* be spending your time—not just at work, but also in every part of your life. The quality of your life is directly affected by how and where you spend your time.

In this day and age, just about everyone feels overwhelmed by all the demands on their time. Those demands have become more intense than ever. Most people are required to do more at work, and that, coupled with their multiple responsibilities outside of work, can be so stressful that they simply feel out of control. And that is one of the worst feelings we can have. It is not the stress that kills you; it's the *distress* from feeling out of control.

But here's one of the most important things I've learned: **Most people are not overworked … they are under-organized.**

We need to figure out how to be more organized, so we can get all the urgent, vital and important things done before it's too late. I believe that the average person can do 50 percent more than they are doing now, including all the *right* things, if they have an effective system for keeping their lives under control.

The number one excuse people use for not getting done what should be done is, **"I did not have enough time."** Throughout this book I will show you why that is a ridiculous statement. It is really nothing more than an excuse, since we all have exactly the same amount of time. Think for a moment about how profound that statement is. It means that Oprah, Bill Gates, Mark Zuckerberg and J.K. Rowling have no more time available to them than what is afforded to you and me. The same is true of every successful person throughout history who's become a household name: Thomas Edison, Susan B. Anthony, Martin Luther King Jr., Estée Lauder—no one has more than 24 hours in a day … and no one has *less* than that either.

Simply put, some very busy people get it all done, and some people who are not all that busy don't get much done.

The problem is, people believe the "I don't have enough time" excuse. They really believe that's just the way it is. But *nothing* is just the way it is. Things are the way you let them be. Again, **we all have the same amount of time.** In my experience, people usually have time to do what they want to do, but they don't make time to do what they *should* do.

As I always tell leaders, *"Your role is to do what has to be done, when it has to be done, in the way it should be done, whether you like it or not and whether they like it or not."* And leadership is not about titles, or job descriptions, or salary grade. There's a big difference between leadership and management. Management is about how to do. **Leadership is about how to be.** It's about having influence and making an impact on others. And leadership is not just for the workplace. **We are all leaders.** In one way or another, whether in business, with our families, neighborhoods, communities or our places of worship, we are all leaders, and we need to be much better organized and much more reliable.

Parents should pay particular attention to this idea. Children are not supposed to be happy all the time. Your responsibility as a parent is to do what has to be done, when it has to be done, in the way it should be done, whether your children like it or not. Turn that TV off. Get them to put away the electronic games and computers.

Get them to play outside and to read books, whether they like it or not. Physical fitness and a love of reading are among the most important gifts you can give your children.

Parents are allowed to say "no." In fact, if you love your kids you will say "no" often, for their own good. Recently, San Francisco tried to impose a law on McDonald's to eliminate the toy in their kiddie meals. I thought that was a joke. The toy is not the problem. The nutritional content of the food is not the problem. *Parents* are the problem. It's not McDonald's fault that so many people are overweight. It's the individual's fault. It stems from a lack of self-discipline. With self-discipline almost anything can be achieved in every aspect of life.

Think of all the leaders who have had a big impact on the world over the centuries. Most of them were not General Managers or Executive Vice Presidents or Presidents. They were not CEOs, CFOs, CIOs, COOs, CMOs, CPOs or any other chiefs you can think of. They were individuals who were committed to what they were doing. They were willing to go all the way. They were passionate, highly focused and relentless. They had a can-do attitude. They never gave up.

I think of people like Harriet Beecher Stowe, Nelson Mandela, Marie Curie, Albert Einstein, Mahatma

Gandhi, Rosa Parks—they were ordinary people when they started, and they left the world a much better place. Think about Abraham Lincoln. Without his focus and determination, the 13th Amendment of our Constitution would not have passed, and the curse of slavery would have persisted. He and the others did what most people said could not be done. They didn't believe them. And as Henry Ford said, "Whether you think you can or you think you can't, you're right."

Never underestimate what a difference you can make. And don't say you don't have the time. You have the same amount of time as all those people whose achievements we celebrate. This book will help you manage that time to accomplish everything you care about. If you are already a disciplined person,

"Efficient" is being able to get things done. "Effective" is doing the right things in the right order, and making sure you address everything that is urgent, vital and important, in every part of your life.

you will learn how to channel that discipline into being even more efficient and more effective. Being both efficient and effective is the name of the game.

"Efficient" is being able to get things done. "Effective" is doing the right things in the right order, and making sure you address everything that is urgent, vital and important, in every part of your life.

Pay Now or Pay Later

Before I took a time management seminar over thirty years ago, I was putting in way too many hours at work. I was regularly working Saturdays and Sundays and taking work home every night. I got the work done, and I considered myself very well organized. But I had very little balance in my life. Then I took the course, and I learned a system that changed my life. As soon as I started using what I learned, I was rewarded, and I've been rewarded every day since.

That's why I wrote this book: so you can benefit from what I've learned. It will reward you in ways you have never imagined. You may feel overwhelmed now. You may feel hopeless because there's too much to do and too little time to do it. Those feelings will disappear in time. It is not hopeless. You can learn to be more organized and disciplined—but you have to want to.

People ask me what I worry about, and I can tell you that one thing I worry about is how disorganized people are.

It is really quite a problem. Most people have absolutely no system in place for how to plan their day, week, month or year. They come to their workplace and follow systems to accomplish their work, like using checklists and following operating guidelines, policies and procedures. When it comes to managing their personal lives though, they have no system. They hope, wish and pray that everything will work out, but that is not a system. In fact, sadly, ***most people actually do a better job of managing time for their organization than they do for themselves.***

I always ask people in my Time/Life Management class one question, and they always get the answer right. The question is, ***"Who is most responsible for controlling the events in your life?"***

You know the answer, and it's the first word in this sentence: **YOU!** I hope this book and approach will help you think about your responsibilities at work, at home and in all other aspects of your life, such as your health, your work in your community, your own personal development and your finances.

Speaking of which, one aspect of managing time is to think both short-term and long-term, and that means developing a retirement plan early enough in life to get the magic of compound interest working in your favor. You can't start to focus on your retirement funds a few years before you want to retire, just as you can't start planning for your children's education when they are sixteen, or thinking about your healthcare needs only when you get sick.

The sad thing is that most people put such responsibilities off until they're forced to deal with them. They start working out after they have bypass surgery. They don't do weight-bearing exercise until they fall and break a hip. They stop smoking only after they're diagnosed with lung cancer. They don't plan for their children's personal development until they get accepted to a college they can't afford, or something much worse happens, like their kids have drug problems, or an unwanted pregnancy, or suffer from low self-esteem and lack of confidence. And they don't think seriously about funding their own retirement until they're 64, so they end up working into their seventies and eighties, and maybe suffering unnecessarily because they can't pay for medical care. Do you plan on being the first human in recorded history to not age and not need retirement funds?

You either pay now or pay later with just about every decision you make about where and how you spend your time.

The Most Crucial Skill

Everyone knows what he or she should and should not be doing, but for some reason many of us don't act on that knowledge. "Someday" is not a day of the week. There may be many psychological reasons why people don't do what they know they should do, but one primary reason is this: ***they just don't know how.*** They have no organized way to get done what should be done. High schools, colleges and universities do not teach courses on time/life management, and frankly it's probably the most crucial skill a person needs to be successful and happy.

At the risk of being repetitive I want to make sure you don't overlook the profundity of this concept, so I am going to state it again:

Time/life management is probably the most crucial skill a person needs to be successful and happy.

I hope this book will turn the light on for you before it is too late. To make the best use of it, you need to be *honest* with yourself.

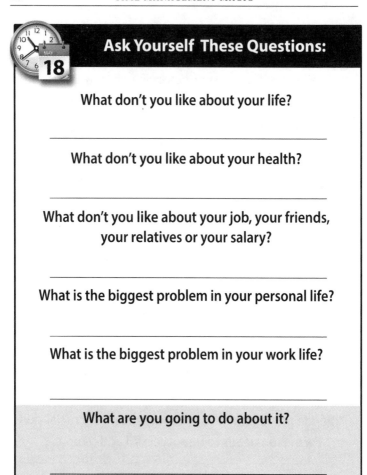

Ask Yourself These Questions:

What don't you like about your life?

_____

What don't you like about your health?

_____

What don't you like about your job, your friends, your relatives or your salary?

_____

What is the biggest problem in your personal life?

_____

What is the biggest problem in your work life?

_____

What are you going to do about it?

_____

Learning the art and science of Time/Life Management will definitely help you fix these problems. But let's be honest, it might not be enough, and if it's not, I urge you to find someone who can help you.

The Day-Timer®

I teach my Time/Life Management course the old-fashioned, pre-digital way. I use a Day-Timer® as the planner for implementing the principles and techniques in the course. The type I use is called the *Two-Page-Per-Day Original*—product number *98010*. The Day-Timer® phone number is 800-225-5005. They will ship directly to you. You can also go directly to their website, www. daytimer.com, to learn more about their products, and for contact information in and outside the United States.

I have been using the Day-Timer® system for over thirty-five years. It is one of the main reasons I have been able to bring balance and order to my hectic days and more success than I ever imagined in both my personal life and my business life. I use my Day-Timer® for planning each day, week and year. I use it to keep my life under control.

I assure you, I am not a dinosaur. I am very comfortable with digital technology, and I celebrate every technological advance. I have a smartphone, and I use it for my calendar, my e-mail, my contact list (over 3,000 contacts) and searching the Web. I don't *need* a smartphone to be organized; I learned to be well organized back when Steve Jobs was dreaming up Apple. But I must admit my smartphone has made me even *more* efficient than I already was.

So I now have two excellent tools for keeping my life under control: my Day-Timer® and my smartphone. Later in this book I will explain how I use both tools to stay organized and keep my life under control even as I travel around the world giving speeches, talks and workshops while also trying to be the best father, grandfather and husband I can be.

From my first-hand observations of thousands of people all around the globe, I am convinced that people who once used a paper pocket day planner and then switched to a smartphone *only* are now less organized, less effective and less efficient than they used to be. One reason is that they waste more time than they've gained because they now have a fancy new toy to play with instead of doing what needs to be done.

I am convinced that people who once used a paper pocket day planner and then switched to a smartphone *only* are now less organized, less effective and less efficient than they used to be.

Very few are disciplined enough to stay focused on what is important instead of what is merely fun, informative or exciting. If you aspire to excellent time management, you can't let yourself become distracted by the endless waves of Facebook, Twitter, Instagram, texts, e-mails and other updates that sidetrack so many aspiring leaders.

Getting Started

The first thing we need to do is define what time management is. For our purposes, let's define "**time**" as *events occurring one after another 24/7*. This simply means that we wake up in the morning and go through a series of events throughout the day, and we repeat this pattern day after day for our entire life. Many of these events we know about when we wake up. We have intentionally set aside time for them and have scheduled them in our appointment calendars.

Other events that occur are simple habits like brushing our teeth, taking our vitamins and kissing our kids goodbye—things we do without the need for scheduling.

You don't need to schedule your habits if they are truly good habits, and you do them without a reminder.

There are also things we want to do, or know we *should* do, like get regular exercise or read to our children before bed, but we don't make enough time for them.

My advice is to start today to schedule those events, just like you schedule a medical checkup or a business meeting. Yes, today! Schedule the priorities in your life.

At one point, I used my Day-Timer® to remind me to drink more water and to call my mother every Sunday. I lost the need for scheduling when drinking water became a natural habit and those Sunday calls became routine.

There is another category of events: things we can't know about in advance because they come up unpredictably and we have to respond to them. Later in the book I will show you how to make sure you have time for those unexpected events and how to handle them so they turn out better.

Now let's look at the second word in "time management." Management is the act of controlling. With time management we are simply trying to keep under control everything we need to manage. If you run a restaurant, for example, your main responsibility is to keep that restaurant under control. That means that when guests/customers arrive, the parking lot is clean, the landscape is attractive, the employees greet them politely and seat them promptly, the server comes to their table at just the right time and knows about all aspects of the menu and wine list. It means that the food arrives promptly, looks great and tastes delicious. It means that the entire restaurant is clean, the lights and music are at just the right levels, and everything else is in good working order. It means that safe work habits are followed and safe, wholesome food is served. It means that employees receive excellent training, development and leadership, feel involved in the business, and are appreciated and respected. It means that when diners are ready, their check comes promptly, and when they leave they are given a nice farewell. Give them all that and they'll be eager to come back.

The restaurant I've just described is under control. But, as anyone who has run a successful business *of any kind* can tell you, that level of excellence can only be achieved if everything in the organization, from expenses to employee morale, is controlled by well-organized leaders through the diligent implementation of checklists, outstanding training procedures and relentless follow-up.

Managing our lives requires the same level of diligence. We've all seen what happens when things are out of control, whether it's a bad theatrical performance, or a bureaucratic snafu in a large organization, or a dry cleaner that loses your shirts, or a meeting where everyone argues and no decisions get made, or a family that can't corral their kids and gets to the game an hour late. Whenever something is out of control it's because of a leadership/management problem, whether the leader is a CEO, an athletic coach, a small business owner or a parent. When it comes to your personal life, *you* are the leader. Don't be a leader who is out of control!

Now that we've defined both "time" and "management," the question is: what is the definition of "time management"? It's simple:

"Time Management" is the act of controlling the events in your life.

Controlling the Uncontrollable

A lot of people would reject that definition because they believe we *can't* control the events in our lives, because so much of what we deal with every day springs up unexpectedly, seemingly out of nowhere. While that is

How to Gain a High Level of Control:

1. **Surround Yourself with Great People**

2. **Train and Educate**

3. **Be Crystal Clear About Your Expectations**

4. **Anticipate and Practice**

5. **Leave Spaces in Your Calendar**

6. **Do It Now!**

pected far more than you think you can.

Here are some practical tips that will give you a high level of control:

1. *Surround yourself with great people.* Some people handle the unexpected better than others. So, if you run an organization or are in charge of a team, always hire and promote outstanding people. That is one of your most important responsibilities as a leader/manager.

Hire skilled people with passion for their work and a can-do attitude. You'd be shocked at how many organizations get disappointing results simply because they hire the wrong people, and then make things worse by not taking action when they fail to perform.

At *Disney*, we didn't have time to manage 40,000 under-performers, and we didn't just hire based on our gut feelings, because our guests deserved to have a wonderful experience at every moment of their visit. In order to ensure operational excellence we had to develop a systematic approach to hiring. You do too. So, save yourself some time and visit www.HireAuthority.com. There, my partner Carol Quinn and I describe the best practices for interviewing potential candidates that will ensure that you hire the best possible people. The site is a real wake-up call.

This topic is also covered in detail in Rule #9 in my book, *The Customer Rules: The 39 Essential Rules for Delivering Sensational Service.*

2. Train and educate. After you hire great people, train them thoroughly and educate them about every aspect of your operation, including your values, your philosophy, your priorities and your mission. Then, when something happens, they will figure out the right solution whether you are physically present or not. Even great people make poor decisions if they are not well trained, because they do not have the appropriate skills and know-how. And don't forget the crucial aspect of testing, to make sure the training has been internalized; and enforcement, to ensure consistency, follow-through and accountability.

3. Be crystal clear about your expectations—for yourself and others. Just as parents have to let their children know exactly what is expected of them, leaders need to communicate their expectations with unambiguous clarity. When you are not 100% clear with your children, your team or your employees, you are going to be disappointed in the outcome more often than not. But if you *are* crystal clear, they will always know what is expected of them, no matter what shocks and surprises come their way.

Don't be wishy-washy. Don't leave room for loopholes. Don't make it possible for people to say, "I did not understand what you meant," or "I did not know when you wanted it," or "I thought you meant such-and-such."

4. *Anticipate and practice.* Think through all the things that can happen and practice how you will handle them. By imagining every possible scenario before they arise, you can plan for what you will do *if* this or that occurs. You can also implement procedures that reduce the likelihood of worst-case scenarios happening in the first place.

For example, at *Disney World*, we understood that hurricanes often strike Central Florida with tremendous force, so we planned for that possibility. We were ready for anything. We trained every Cast Member, and we had all of the necessary supplies on hand. No one can keep a hurricane from coming, but we could be as prepared as possible, to minimize the damage and loss of life.

Similarly, my wife Priscilla and I have anticipated that a tornado could strike our house. Among other things, we know which room we will both run to if we have only twenty seconds to get to a safer place. We know that being surprised by an actual tornado is not exactly the best time to hold a meeting on which room we should go to.

Having a conversation with your family on what to do in case of a fire is good anticipation. Teaching your children to swim and putting a safety fence around your pool is another example. And as your kids get older, you and your spouse can anticipate what you will do about difficult subjects like drugs and sex. Taking CPR training is excellent anticipation. So is driving a comfortable distance behind other cars, and planning financially for continuing education and retirement.

If you're a business leader, you can anticipate all the possible needs and demands of your future customers. Then you can put into place solutions for all contingencies, with appropriate training procedures and operating guidelines for your employees. That way you won't get complaints about your business opening later than advertised, or the bathrooms not being clean, or employees who text instead of focusing on customers.

I often compare business performance to putting on a play. If you're going to be ready when the curtain goes up, you should write out a script for every function and every contingency, and then make sure you and your cast rehearse your roles thoroughly. That way you can ensure that you'll be able to control the uncontrollable. You'll find great advice about this in Rule #10 and Rule #12 in my book, *The Customer Rules*.

5. *Leave spaces in your calendar.* Perhaps the most important thing you have to have when something unanticipated crops up is the very subject of this book–TIME. You've already seen how much I believe in scheduling everything meaningful in your life. But it's also important not to impose commitments on every minute of your day, or else you won't have the flexibility to respond when stuff happens. That's why I've always been as meticulous about penciling in free, uncommitted periods in my planner every day. Those gaps give me space to move things around if I need to spontaneously deal with the unexpected, whether it's a crisis or an opportunity. And if nothing arises that must be dealt with right away, I have plenty of items on my to-do lists to use that open time effectively.

6. *Do it now.* As you're about to see, having a planning system is powerful and crucial. However, I must add this: many things have to be done even if they're not written in your planner. Sometimes you are faced with a decision or problem that can't be foreseen, and you have to act, whether you want to or not. So, I want to share with you a simple mental technique I learned thirty-five years ago and adopted as a habit. It's called *"DO IT NOW."* When I know there's something I have to do, especially if I don't want to do it, I just remember that phrase: *"DO IT NOW."* Then I do it. Now!

Speaking of doing things *now*, one thing you should do right away, before moving on to chapter 2, is contemplate how you currently spend your time, how you should be spending your time and where you should *stop* spending your time. You will find it a good use of time to take a walk or sit in silence and think about these questions:

Ask Yourself These Questions:

• *Are you getting real value out of everything you spend your time on?*

• *Is the way you now spend your time going to help you achieve your goals and realize your dreams? (Don't forget: the difference between dreams and nightmares rests totally with you!)*

• *Of all the responsibilities you have taken on, which ones should you get to work on right away?*

• *What should you start doing now that won't pay off for 1, 5, 10, 20 or even 40 years?*

• *What did you do yesterday that you need to go back and do better?*

*"Dost thou love life?
Then do not squander time,
for it is the stuff that life is made of."*

BENJAMIN FRANKLIN

CHAPTER 2

It's Your Time... and Your Life!

Now that you've started to think about how you spend your time, you're on the road to learning something that will increase your personal satisfaction and overall happiness. This chapter will get into some of the nuts and bolts of how to organize your life in a more systematic way.

Routine is important. That is why operating guidelines, checklists, daily systems, policies and procedures are frequently referenced and consistently stressed in any successful organization. *Marriott* and *Disney* are two excellent examples of this. Have you often referenced and consistently stressed operating guidelines, checklists, daily systems, policies and procedures in your organization? Remember, you can't have a successful organization if you are plagued by disorganization and lack of consistent performance.

Now, assuming that you and your organization do indeed have those crucial elements in place, you can make things even more productive and efficient with a system for planning your day that helps make sure you get the right things done at the right time. That's what you're about to learn. I assure you it will be well worth your time—and your time is what this book is all about.

Is the system perfect? No, it is not! However, it's as good as it gets, and by following this system you will be better off than most people in the world. The vast majority have no idea what they should be working on at any given moment, and very few have a system in place to get the important things done.

Knowing what to do and doing it are two different things. That may sound obvious, but you'd be surprised how many people don't live as though it's obvious. They know what they should be doing, but they don't have a system, a set of habits or a solid routine for getting those things done—especially things that pay off down the road. Many of us sit around wishing, hoping and praying that things work out, but we all know that most wishes don't come true, many hopes don't materialize and many prayers are not answered. It takes good planning and effective action. I suggest that you write down your three biggest wishes, and your primary hopes and all the things you pray for. Then see if you can use the system you're about to learn and make them all come true.

Are you reluctant to get more systematic about your time management? Do you need to be convinced to learn a system? Think about this:

How do you feel at the end of a day when you had ten things to get done and you didn't do any of them, or most of them? Not very good, right? And how do you feel if you continue to not get important things done day after day and week after week? This is not a trick question. The answer is simple. You feel depressed, distressed and just plain awful. And as we know from medical experiments, those feelings are very bad for your health.

Now ask yourself this: How do you feel on a day when you have a lot to do and you *do it all*? When you get done all the things that need to be done? Again, this is not a trick question. You feel great, don't you? You feel happy. You feel confident. And perhaps most important of all, you feel ready and able to take on more.

Having a System Is Vital

Have you ever been in a meeting where a manager says something like this? "I need one of you to volunteer to take on this project. It will take about one day of your time each week for the next few months. Who would like to do it?" Usually, the whole room goes silent, and most people look down because they don't want to be noticed.
You can practically hear everyone praying that they

won't have to be the one to take on the assignment. That's why people, like students, tend to sit in any row except the front row, so the boss (or teacher) can't see them.

Then, all of a sudden, someone raises his or her hand and says, "I'll take that on. I can do that." And who is the person who volunteers? Most of the time it is one of the busiest people in the room. I'll tell you something else about the people who volunteer. They are not only extremely busy already, but they usually won't be around very long. Why? Because they are going to get promoted or hired away by another organization that sees a star in the making.

That person should be *you*.

What I just described takes place not only in business organizations, but also in neighborhoods, places of worship, nonprofit volunteer groups, and everywhere people come together to accomplish goals. A few busy people raise their hands and take on even more responsibility, while everyone else wonders how they manage to do it. I'll tell you how. They have a system. They may or may not be conscious of it, but they have *a systematic way of working*. And they know they can fit anything into that system. They never have excuses like "I'm too busy," or "I don't have time," or "We can't do that because our resources are all tied up."

Having a system is the name of the game. As the leaders of Southwest Airlines said, "There is a best way to land a plane. Let's do it that way."

Are you convinced now?

Let me add another advantage to having an organizational system in place. Think of it as a tremendous fringe benefit. When you start getting more done, the rewards are not just material; they're mental and emotional as well. You start to realize that **you can accomplish anything**. This boosts your self-confidence and self-esteem, and that leads directly to higher and higher levels of performance and self-satisfaction. It becomes a virtuous cycle. The stronger your self-esteem and self-confidence become, the better you perform and the more you accomplish—which raises confidence and self-esteem another notch.

At the Controls

The issue of what we can and cannot control is a big part of time management. Here is a concise synopsis:

There are events we can control and events we can't control. We cannot control things like the weather, or war, or the economy. Where the uncontrollable is concerned, we need to learn how to adapt to the new conditions.

There are also events in life that we can't stop from happening, but that we can control to some extent by being prepared. As I mentioned earlier, we can do that by surrounding ourselves with great people, anticipating scenarios in advance, training and practicing for all contingencies, maintaining our physical and mental health, and so forth.

Then there are events we can control, but may choose not to. Examples can include our health, our weight, our capacity for learning new things, our retirement funds, our friendships and intimate relationships, just to name a few.

Another category? Things we think we can control, but we actually can't. Changing other people is a big one. As many married people will testify, it's usually futile to try turning another person's weaknesses into strengths, or to try changing an introvert into an extrovert. During the first half of my marriage I tried to get Priscilla to be more like me. I wanted her to have a day planner like I did. She said she didn't need one. If she wanted something done she would put it in *my* day planner. I wanted her closet to be organized like mine. She told me to stay out of her closet. It took a while, but I finally learned that she is Priscilla, and I am Lee, and the only one of those two I can control is Lee. Which led to an extremely important lesson. When I changed Lee, lo and behold,

Priscilla got better.

Finally, there are events we think we can control, and we do. That happens when we take responsibility for our lives and seize control of our savings, our relationships with others, our health and so on, including *our time*.

So stop wasting your time and getting frustrated for no reason. Forget about things you can't control. Identify what you *can* control. Focus on those things, and you will see big results.

The Balancing Act

A good time management system should help us create balance in our lives.

People erect artificial barriers between work and home, but the truth is, if you are having problems at work, you will also have problems at home, and if you are having problems at home, you will also have problems at work. My advice is to think about your life *in its entirety* every day.

A good way to start is to make a list of all your areas of responsibility, in all the different parts of your life, as a spouse or life partner, as a parent to your children, as a child to your parents, as a boss to your employees or direct reports; as an employee of your company or the owner of your own company; as a member of a religious community, as a citizen of a neighborhood, a city, a state, a nation and a planet, and as an individual responsible for your own health, your own retirement plan, your continual learning plan, and on and on. All of these roles and responsibilities, which continually change throughout your life, should be treated as an integrated whole in your time management plan.

"Failing to plan is planning to fail."

That quote has been attributed to many people, but whoever said it was very wise indeed. One of the first, and maybe most important, aspects of a good time management system is to take time for planning *every single day*.

Plan each day as diligently as you plan your vacations. You wouldn't wake up one morning and take off for a vacation without a plan for where you want to go and what you want to see and do. So why start a typical day with no plan? Think of it as a GPS or a map–without it you will not get to where you want to go. In fact, without a plan you might not even know where you want to go.

This simply means setting aside anywhere from a few minutes to a half hour every day to think about what you need to get done. Not just this day, but this week, this month, and if you're really good at planning, this year and the years to follow. I am talking about real planning: taking your day planner and a pencil and writing down all the things you need to get done as they pop into your mind. Some tasks may be right for today's list, some for tomorrow's, and others for next month's or even further ahead. The point is, you need to have a systematic way to write things in an appropriate place as you think of them. Writing down to-do items dramatically increases your odds of actually getting them done.

You just need to find a quiet place in the morning, or the evening before, to write down your thoughts and plans in your to-do list, whether in a day planner, a computer or a smartphone. Sometimes, when I return from vacation, I need an hour or more of planning time to get everything lined up for the coming days and weeks.

Here are a few suggestions about the kinds of things you'll want to think about as you put your plan together.

Consider These Areas When Planning:

- *Job Responsibilities*

- *House/Home Responsibilities*

- *Family Responsibilities*

- *Place-of-Worship Responsibilities*

- *Community Responsibilities*

- *Financial Responsibilities (investments, retirement planning and timing, etc.)*

- *Health Responsibilities (diet, exercise, medical, relaxation, sleep)*

- *Social Responsibilities (entertaining, relationship building, social activities)*

- *Commitments to others*

- *Communication (correspondence, meetings, coaching, counseling, birthdays, anniversaries, etc.)*

- *Personal Development (reading, courses, school, new experiences, continual learning, www.Thrive15.com)*

I am sure there are many more categories to consider, but this is a good start. When you take five to thirty minutes a day to intentionally plan your life in these areas it becomes very hard to drift too far off of your desired course.

The value of investing that time is incalculable. Yet many people resist doing it. And guess what the main excuse I hear is for not taking the time to plan each day. You guessed it: "I don't have the time." They don't have the time to save time! No time to use time better! That's like saying you need cash but you don't have the time to make a withdrawal. Or like saying you want to get somewhere but you don't have time to stop and get directions. Instead, you waste time driving around in circles, and what is the cost of getting there late—or not at all?

Let me share with you the facts of life. When you think clearly and plan in advance of acting, you save a huge amount of time. Not only that, but you work on the right things in the right order. I learned this the hard way. I used to go to work and look for something easy to do. Then I learned it was better to do things in the order of the priority that they needed to get done. As a result, my life and career changed radically for the better. But don't just take my word for it, try it and see for yourself.

Priorities, Priorities, Priorities

There are Three Levels of Priority:
- Urgent
- Vital
- Important

Of course, there are also low-value priorities, but you don't need to deal with them since the top three will keep you plenty busy.

Here's another excuse I hear from people who resist organizing their time systematically: "I'm too busy putting out fires to take the time to plan." When I hear that, I think, "Where are those people's priorities? Why do they think those fires get started in the first place?" Largely because they didn't plan!

Think of planning as fire prevention. Wouldn't you prefer to prevent fires instead of fighting them? It's like taking the time to exercise: you invest time to feel better and prevent disease, and as a result you save the time and cost of treating serious illnesses.

The other excuse I hear is, "Having this big plan every day limits my freedom." Again, priorities! It's true that planning limits your freedom—your freedom to waste time. If you don't want to do anything, then plan on doing nothing. That's definitely an option. Sometimes, doing nothing is a top priority. Often, on a Saturday or Sunday, I don't have one single item in my Day-Timer® because I've decided to just chill out that day.

If you don't think prioritizing time for planning is a good idea, think of life-and-death situations, like war. Having worked with high-ranking officers in the American armed forces, I can assure you they all agree–the better the planning, the shorter the war. It is like that with all projects, whether large or small. Take the time to plan your vacation far in advance, for example, and you will get the flights and hotels you want at a better price, not to mention avoid all kinds of hassles that can ruin your vacation.

Coming Attractions

In the pages that follow, we will take a look at the Day-Timer® **Monthly Planner Books**, where you can record your calendar of scheduled events and appointments, plan your work in the *"To Be Done Today"* section for business and personal goals, record your phone messages and phone numbers for return calls and record personal observations and thoughts in the diary section for future follow-up.

We will also look at the **Advance Planner** section of the Day-Timer® and discuss how to use it to plan longer-term activities such as your vacation and medical checkups, so you can, on a moment's notice, review your calendar far into the future. We will also briefly review the **Address and Phone Directory**, which you can use in addition to your smartphone contact list.

Every aspect of your life will benefit from implementing this system. Yes, it does take self-discipline and commitment, as do all worthwhile things in this short life we have here on earth. It is not easy to change any habit, but hard things become easy if you just get started and practice day after day. Learning to ride a bike was hard for me. Learning to be a public speaker was hard for me. Learning how to write books was hard for me. When you focus on something that you really want to accomplish, it does not take long to turn a bad habit into a good habit. You can do it, and the return on your investment will be tremendous.

"Until you value yourself, you will not value your time. Until you value your time, you will not do anything with it."

M. SCOTT PECK

CHAPTER 3

How to Use a Day-Timer® Daily Planner

Let's get right into how to use the Day-Timer® to plan your life on a daily basis. I have used this system for thirty-five years, and it's still indispensable. It fits into my back pocket, and it goes everywhere I go. I use it so much that Priscilla complains that I hold hands with my planner and my phone more than with her. I sometimes call my planner my "second brain." Unlike the one in my head, it remembers everything I put into it.

There are three parts to the Day-Timer® system. **They are: 1) Advance Planner** (18 Months), 2) **Monthly Planner** (Day-by-Day), 3) **Telephone Directory**.

You can see examples of the Advance Planner on the next page and the Monthly Planner on page 64-65. Refer to those illustrations as you learn how to use the system.

You will see as you look at the Advance Planner that this is a place to schedule both the business and private events in your life, from picking someone up at the

Advance Planner

SUNDAY	MONDAY	TUESDAY	WEDNESDAY
	6:15 OFFICE 9-11 SC	6:15 OPT	6:15 OPT
		8 - ERIN/KARL	8-8:15 JOHN ROGERS
	12- DIETER		9- JAMES R
	2- JANE	3- 80	3- DT DISNEY
	5:15 EXERCISE	5:15 E	5:15 E
1		**2**	**3**
	6:15 OPT	6:15 OPT	6:15 OPT
8 - TO NOT DOSA	9-11 SC	8 - KARL/ERIN	10 - ROGER
	12-GRACE COFFEE	10- MK WHEEL	12 - GEORGE
		12 - WALK MGM	3:30 - BUD
4 - E	5:15 EXERCISE	5:15 E	5:15 E
7	**8**	**9**	**10**
	6:15 OPT	6:15 OPT	6:15 OPT
	9-11 SC	8 - KARL/ERIN	9 - SUE MASON
	12-3 VPOC		
		12 - 2 EMMIC?	2- MARGOT SCHOOL
4 - E			
	5:15 EXERCISE	5:15 E	5:15 E
14	**15**	**16**	**17**
	6:15 OPT	6:15 OPT	6:15 OPT
	8 -9 WRITE SPEECH	8 - KARL/ERIN	
	10 - JOHN J.	10 - WALK MK	10- KEVIN
			CALL CENTER
8 - 12 MK	12 - BILL		
WITH KIDS	3 - DIETER		
	5- EXERCISE	5- E	5- E
21	**22**	**23**	**24**
	DALLAS	6:15 OPT	8:15 OPT
DALLAS	HOLIDAY	8 - KARL/ERIN	
		10- HR MEETING	12-AL
		1-SAMS	2- F MEETING
	3 AA#1257	3- BILL S.	3 - JIM K.
	TO ORLANDO		
7- DINNER	SEAT 21 C&D		
28	**29**	**30**	**31**

April

S	M	T	W	T	F	S
						1
2	3	4	5	6	7	8
9	10	11	12	13	14	15
16	17	18	19	20	21	22
23	24	25	26	27	28	29
30						

THURSDAY	FRIDAY	SATURDAY
6:15 OPT	6:15 OPT	
	10-12 VISTA WAY	10 COSTCO
		4 - WORKOUT
5:15 E	5:15 E	7 - DINNER
		JAKES
4	**5**	**6**
6:15 OPT	6:15 OPT	
10 - WALK EPCOT	8 - W/EXEC COMM	
3 - RICH		
4 - JOHN	4 - E	4 - EXERCISE
5:15 E	6:30 UW DINNER	9 - MOVIE
11	**12**	**13**
6:15 OPT	6:15 OPT	
8 - KARL/ERIN	10 - WORKOUT	
10 - DAK		
11:30 - AL	12:30-4:30 TIME MGT.	12 - ART SHOW
1 - PHYSICAL		
4 - MARY POP		
5:15 WORKOUT	5 - TO BEACH	5 - EXERCISE
7:30 - JAMES **18**	V-DINNER **19**	BABYSIT **20**
6:15 OPT	DALLAS	DALLAS
	VACATION	↓
	DAY	
12 - WORKOUT	12- LUNCH	12 - JERRY/BARBARA
4 - MARY POP	4-WORKOUT	
6 AA #1247 DFW	6:30-DINNER	5 -NANCY/WALDO
SEAT 12 A&B **25**	MARY'S **26**	7-DINNER **27**

M A Y

NOTES

June

S	M	T	W	T	F	S
				1	2	3
4	5	6	7	8	9	10
11	12	13	14	15	16	17
18	19	20	21	22	23	24
25	26	27	28	29	30	

airport to your annual physical, from a meeting at work to a dinner with a client or friend. The **Advance Planner** has 18 months in it so that in a few seconds you can record a scheduled event or an appointment up to a year and a half in the future. Plus, it actually has a place on the back pages to schedule things up to *five years* in the future. That's a lot of power in one little book, and there is no battery to go dead on you.

For instance, when I wanted to plan a trip to Hong Kong to see our good friends Don and Suzy Robinson, I used my planner seven months in advance to map out our departure and return dates. Planning ahead enabled me to use my frequent flyer miles to get two free tickets. Many people complain that they have trouble using their frequent flyer miles, but I don't because I plan ahead. I even had my pick of seats since mine was the first reservation for this flight. As a result, Priscilla and I were able to stretch our legs in the exit row seats, a major advantage on a long trip like that.

Here's another example. When I had my annual physical in 2010, my doctor said I should get a colonoscopy again in five years. I flipped right over to 2015 and wrote the next exam in my advance planner. Exams like that are important to me; I consider them life-and-death priorities, and I know that if I forget to have the test or get it a year late and find out I am going to die of cancer because it was not detected early enough, I would wish that I'd had a better system for planning. This terrible scenario does, in fact, happen to many people.

Problems with my teeth are not life threatening, but I take the same approach to my dental checkups. I just had one, and as I left the office I wrote the date and time for the next exam in my **Advance Planner** six months down the road. I recorded it in my smartphone as well, so I'm doubly sure I won't forget or double-book. Now, I don't have to waste energy thinking about my dental checkup, and I don't have to waste time scheduling it later on. This is a good example of "Do It Now."

Now let's turn to the **Monthly Planner**. You can see that it has several sections. (See next page for an example.) The first section, at the top left-hand corner, is for *"Appointments & Scheduled Events."* This is a mirror image of the **Advance Planner**. The example on the next page is for May 18. If you look at the items scheduled for May 18 in both the **Monthly Planner** and the **Advance Planner**, you will see that they are the same. The description in the **Advance Planner** is sometimes a little different because there is less space to write in. *Abbreviations will become easy for you once you start to use this system.*

Monthly Planner

18

APPOINTMENTS & SCHEDULED EVENTS

NAME • PLACE • SUBJECT

HRS.

A.M.

6:15 – 8:00 OFFICE PLANNING TIME
8:00 – WEEKLY UPDATE WITH ERIN & KARL 5/18

10:00 – WALK DAK WITH BETH STEVENS

NOON

P.M.

11:30 – AL UPDATE (5/18 DIARY)

1:00 – 3:00 ANNUAL PHYSICAL (B.)
4-5 PDP REVIEW WITH MARY
5:15 WORKOUT

NTE

7:30 BIRTHDAY DINNER FOR JAMES (5/18 DIARY)

✓ TO BE DONE TODAY (ACTION LIST)

BIRTHDAY NOTE TO RALPH – GRACE
SCHED. MEETING ON PRODUCTIVITY PLAN
WRITE MAIN STREET DIARY FOR JUNE
SCHED VISIT TO CONCIERGE LOUNGES
GIVE ROSEMARY RESTAURANT FEEDBACK (5/17)
THANK YOU NOTE TO JIM
FIX CHECK-IN
FIX BOB

SCHED APPT WITH FINANCIAL ADVISOR
OPEN RETIREMENT SAVINGS ACCT
SCHED YEARLY EYE EXAM
SCHED VISIT TO M.K. WITH CHILDREN
LETTER TO MOTHER
BOOK AIR TICKETS FOR VACATION IN SEPT

EXPENSE & REIMBURSEMENT RECORD:

Item – What?	Where? Duration?	Purpose Who What Involved?	To whom Paid?	Reimbursed? By whom?	Amount
CARL – 407-325-6543					
ELIZ JOHNSON 202-464-3251					GUEST
BILL ROGERS 321-424-1564					CAST
AL – 3464					
FRANK MCMILLAN 407-322-4651					LAWYER.
GRACE – 251-625-8888					THANKS
PRISCILLA – 407-876-3072					

E E E E E E E E E E E E E E E E E E E E E

DIARY AND WORK RECORD

HRS.	NAME OR PROJECT	DESCRIPTION	TIME

8 0800

7:30PM DINNER JAMES HOUSE
1-4 TO LEE RD - TAKE RIGHT
GO 1.4 MILES TO OAK STREET - RIGHT
2 BLOCKS ON LEFT 546 OAK ST.
  407-414-3217 WIFE: JUDY
                KIDS: DAN/MARY

9 0900

10 1000

8:00 ERIN / KARL UPDATE
 - REVIEW CONTINGENCY PLAN
 - DISCUSS ORGAN STRUCTURE
 - THANK THEM

11 1100

11:30 AL WEISS UPDATE
 - ORGAN STRUCTURE
 - OVERTIME
 - CONCERNS / ADVICE

12 1200

* PRISCILLA/GROCERY STORE/PICK UP ON WAY HOME
* MILK, BREAD, NY TIMES, STRAWBERRIES, GRAPES

1 1300

ELIZ. JOHNSON - LEE TO CALL GUEST
 - HAD POOR EXPERIENCE AT CHECK-IN
 - MARY RUDE
 - ROOM 6PM
 - CALL BACK BY 12N FRIDAY 5/19

2 1400

3 1500

4 1600

5 1700

As you can see in this example, I used "E" for exercise. I also used other abbreviations, such as "P" for Priscilla, "M" for Marsha (my secretary at the time), and "OPT" for office and planning time. Also in the **Advance Planner** is a section called "Notes." Here you can put reminders for yourself, so when that month arrives your notes will be waiting for you to let you know what you need to take action on. Good things to put in here are dates you want to remember, like birthdays, or scheduling your annual physical, or … basically anything.

Another section in the **Monthly Planner** is titled "*To Be Done Today.*" This is what to use during **planning time every morning**. Actually, the term "To Be Done Today" is a little misleading; it does not mean that you will definitely get that item done today. What it does mean is that you have the *intention* of getting started on that item today. Some tasks, of course, don't take very long and will get accomplished on the day they're recorded in, while others may take weeks or months to complete.

The third section in the **Monthly Planner** is titled "*Expenses & Reimbursement Record.*" This is in the lower left-hand corner. I actually don't use this for expense notations. Instead, I write down all the phone calls I need to make, including the ones I have to return. This way the phone numbers and names are with me no matter where I am, and when I have a free minute or two I can return a call and check one off of my list. *Saving a minute here and a minute there is part of what time management is all about.* Those wasted minutes really add up. You can pick up an extra hour a day just by having everything you need at your fingertips at all times.

The right-hand section of the **Monthly Planner** is titled *"Diary,"* and that's exactly what it's for. As every diary writer knows, you can write *anything* in your dear diary. This one is no different. You can use it to take notes at a meeting. You can list the items you have to pick up at the supermarket on the way home. You can write the directions to the home you're having dinner at that night. In the example, you can see "Dinner at James' house" at 7:30 p.m.

The ("5/18 Diary") in parentheses means "refer to." When you put parentheses around something like a date or location it tells you to refer to that date or place for more information. In this case, the information consists of the directions to James' home. You will also notice in the *"Diary"* section a list of items I want to remember for my meetings with my direct reports at *Disney*, Karl and Erin, and with my boss, Al, plus some grocery items Priscilla asked me to pick up. Also, in this example are some notes from a *Disney* World guest who called about some service issues I needed to follow up on. As you can see, the Diary is a place to make notes on anything you want to.

The **Telephone Directory** is the other part of this system. I suggest that you take the time to write in every personal and business phone number and address that you need to have with you, wherever you are. I rely on the phone directory for numbers I frequently call, like neighbors, my children's friends, my own friends, my direct reports, credit card companies, doctor, bank, etc. That way, when I need a number it's at my fingertips. Of course, smartphones make looking up numbers and calling even faster—as long as you keep one with you at all times and make sure it's always charged. The Day-Timer® directory serves as a backup system, which gives me comfort. I have redundancy systems in every part of my life, just as airplanes do, so I won't crash. By the way, it's also a great place to keep your pin numbers.

At Your Discretion

We all have *discretionary time*. This is basically when you can do whatever you want, up to a point. "Discretionary" means that it is your decision. If you are a front-line employee, you may not have much discretionary time at work. If your shift is from, say, 8 a.m. to 5 p.m., your only discretionary time during that period is on your breaks. That's when you get to do whatever you want: eat, read, make phone calls, do push-ups, write e-mails, talk with your friends or coworkers, or whatever. Lunch break is just a name, not a requirement to eat for thirty or sixty minutes. The other discretionary time you have is from the minute you get off work at 5 p.m. until you return the next morning, and, of course, on your days off.

I make this point because people are always saying they don't have time to do this or that. But we have a lot of discretionary time on our hands, so it is really a matter of making the right choices. You can exercise or watch television or do both at the same time. This is a personal choice. You can play golf on the weekend, or spend time with your loved ones, or play golf with them. This is a personal choice. You can do the dishes, or read a bedtime story to your kids. This is a personal choice. Reading to your children is time well spent; it will pay off when they have a love of reading, do well in school and become self-sufficient citizens. So often, it is about making the right personal choices, not about having too little time.

Try to make the right choices. If you and your loved ones are in agreement on how to spend your time, then you probably have made the right choices. One friend of mine takes his wife out to dinner and a movie every Wednesday and plays golf all day on Saturday. This works for them because he is giving the right amount of time and attention to both of his loves.

People in different positions within an organization have different amounts of discretionary time during their working hours. A Customer Service Manager has more discretionary time than a line worker. A General Manager has more discretionary time than a Customer Service Manager, and a Vice President has more discretionary time than both. That's how it is. When you retire, you will have loads of discretionary time.

The point is not that as the salary grade increases people have more time to goof off. What it means is they have a lot more latitude to decide how they are going to spend their time and what they are going to work on. Those who make good choices succeed and advance in their industries.

One reason daily planning time is so important is that it gives you a well-thought-out list of things to work on *when you have discretionary time*. It is your list of priorities for work and the rest your life for that day. So, when you are not in a meeting or performing a scheduled task, you can go to this list and knock off one item at a time.

There is a saying that really sheds the right light on planning time: **"Do what you *should* do now so that later you can do what you *want* to do."** This applies to your personal life—to retirement planning, your health, raising your children correctly, etc.—not just your work life.

Planning to Plan

So now you might be thinking, "OK, I understand why planning time is so important. But how do you do it?"

Well, first you find a quiet place, either in your work area or away from your work area if "quiet" does not exist where you work. It can be at home before you leave in the morning, a break room, or the privacy of your car, or a coffee shop.

1. First, take out your day planner and open it to today's date (in our example that's May 18 in the Monthly Planner). There you will find items that you recorded in the past.

2. Go through your business and personal mail and add new entries to your "To Be Done Today" list. Always start at the top, listing business items from top to bottom. Then list personal tasks from bottom to top. This keeps all your business items together and all your personal items together.

Note that you are not listing them in order of priority. We will discuss how to prioritize each item in a moment. Nor are you listing them in the order you will work on them today. For now, just concentrate on getting a list of *"To Be Done Today"* items into your day planner.

3. Look back at yesterday in your day planner to see what you did not get done. Move those items forward, either to today or to another day in the future. The goal is to always list items on the day you feel you are most likely to get them accomplished, taking into consideration how many hours of your day are tied up with scheduled events, appointments and other tasks. Also think about what you could have done better yesterday, and make it better as quickly as possible.

Each of these first three steps will usually add some new items to your *"To Be Done Today"* list. Those steps are the easy part. Step 4 is the hardest and the most important.

4. Think hard about all of those parts of your life that we listed earlier. As you think of things that you need to attend to, want to attend to or must attend to, write them in the business or personal section of "To Be Done Today." You want to think not only about today, but tomorrow, next week, next month, next year, two years from now, five years from now and further into the future.

Ask yourself this question every day: **"What should I do today that will not pay off for 1, 5, 10, 15, 20, 25, 30, 35, 40 or even 50 years from now?"**

Also think about every responsibility that you have signed up for in your life: to your spouse, your partner, your friends, your parents, your children, and to your-self—to your retirement, your health, your career development, and so on. You can then add to the lists for each of the time periods in your "To Be Done Today" list, such as, Today: Call John on report due today. Tomorrow: Review Mary's performance appraisal. Next Week: Plan meetings for the month with my direct reports and plan my September vacation. Next Month: Work on the long-term organizational structure, inventory my personal possessions for insurance, sign up for Lee's Time Management class and visit my children's teachers. Next Year: Schedule all of my annual medical checkups, visit a financial planner and plan to go back to school to get my undergraduate degree. Five Years: Get that medical test I'm supposed to get after fifty and plan a visit to England to see my relatives. Thirty Years: Have enough savings to retire and have a hobby to keep me engaged in life.

Remember, if you don't see that financial planner and start saving and investing, you won't be able to meet your retirement goal thirty years from now. If you don't find out about college programs today, you won't get around to having your degree three or four years from now.

The point is that many things you work on today, this week and this month won't pay off for years. Things like coaching and counseling your direct reports fall into this category, as well as educating your children and taking the time to discipline them as required. You should start planning how to get what you want as soon as you think of it. Then write it down so you don't forget and work at it persistently until you achieve what you decided you wanted to achieve.

By the way, if you are in the fourth step of planning time, **"thinking,"** and you cannot think of anything, I suggest you ask your leader, your direct reports, or your loved ones what they think you should be working on. They will probably give you a list. Recently, I had something that I wanted to change at work, but I could not think of how to do it. Just thinking about it every day for a couple of weeks helped me to finally come up with some ideas. I think they represent a partial solution, and I will now run my thoughts by others to fully develop those ideas.

Don't forget to include exercise in your lists—and not just for the well-known health benefits. An interesting thing happens when you are exercising. I actually get some of my best ideas and insights when I am in the middle of my exercise routine. Jogging or walking has been especially productive over the years for giving me new ideas and creative solutions. I don't know if it is because more blood is pumping through my brain or whether it's the solitude of working out. All I know is, it works.

While we're on the topic, I have learned that the worst excuse for not exercising is that you are too tired.

Most of the time, when you feel tired, exercise will actually re-energize you. It seems to me that the worse I feel, the more I need to exercise. So, when my Day-Timer® says I have an appointment to exercise, I do it, no matter how I feel, because I always keep my appointments with myself. I just start working out, knowing I might come up with a really good idea in the next few minutes. At a minimum, I will be stress-free when I get home and will be more pleasant to be around, and that is a big time-saver.

The next chapter you will learn how to work through the day once you have put a priority on each item in your "To Be Done Today" list.

*See the Monthly Planner on pages 100-101

"To comprehend a man's life, it is necessary to know what he does but also what he purposely leaves undone."

JOHN HALL GLADSTONE

CHAPTER 4

Assigning Right Priorities
Urgent, Vital & Important!

So far, we've discussed how to think about your responsibility in managing your time and your life. You are the key here.

· *We talked about how to use planning time and which areas of your life to think about as you are doing it.*

· *We talked about the importance of having only one calendar for both business and personal items.*

· *We talked about how well the Day-Timer® works because its three sections cover all the things you need. It is like having an office in your pocket.*

Now that you know how to make lists of things to do and how to use the Day-Timer® to become more efficient, let's look at how to put the right priorities on each item in your daily list so you are not only efficient but also *effective.*

How to Prioritize:

- *URGENT first*
- *Vital next*
- *Important after that*
- Low value last, if ever

Use these priority categories to finalize your plan for the day. On pages 100-101 you can see the same list of things to do on May 18 that was in the previous chapter, but with a difference: before, it was just a list; now each item has a priority assigned to it. It's only when you finish putting the priority on each item that you have a real plan!

Doing things in the right order is very important.

I used to come home and turn on the TV. Priscilla would start talking to me. But I was preoccupied with the TV, and that turned out to be a problem. I realized that listening to the person you live with is extremely important, so I rearranged my priorities. Now I come home, tell Priscilla I love her, give her a kiss, listen to everything she has to say, and only then do I turn on the TV. The right order really does make a difference in results.

I did the same thing at work. I learned early in my career to start the day by going around and touching base with everyone on my team, face-to-face. Only then did I dive into what awaited me on my computer or the pile of papers on my desk. I strongly urge you to do the same:

Touch your team before you touch your work.

When it comes to priorities, timing matters. Doing the right thing too late is a problem. That's why it's vital to apologize fast, and to tell the truth the first time. Tell your loved ones you love them before they have to ask. Tell your team members how much you appreciate them and why, before they quit because they feel unappreciated. And do it often. Everyone wants to know they matter, and when they know it, they're more committed and loyal.

Having the ability to focus on and accomplish your priorities in the right order is the name of the game for effectiveness.

So, here's what to do. If something is:

- **URGENT**, put an asterisk (*) next to it.
- *Vital*, put an **A** next to it.
- **Important**, put a **B** next to it.
- Limited value, put a **C** next to it.

Which do you do first? The **URGENT**, of course, because you, your boss, a customer, an employee, or someone else has decided that it is **URGENT**.

What do you do if you have several **URGENT** tasks? You have to decide which is the *most* **URGENT**. Number them from most **URGENT** to least **URGENT**, starting with number 1.

What about URGENT tasks that you are unable to complete that day? Your most URGENT personal and business tasks should be in your planner *every day*, no matter how long it takes.

After you finish **URGENT** matters, turn to the *Vital* group. *Vital* items may be things that will take you six months, one year or longer to complete, but when you do get them done they create great value in everything from customer satisfaction, employee morale, business results and even personal relationships.

This concept is important to understand. Most people don't get started on *Vital* tasks *today* because they often seem overwhelming. But we are talking about *getting started* today, not finishing today. These big, *Vital* items are usually tasks that take a long time to complete, but have a big payoff.

You'll probably have many items on your *Vital* list. As with the **URGENT** tasks, number them in order of priority. After you get started on the *Vital* issues and do all you can on them for today, make sure the incomplete items are also on your next day's list.

Now, move on to the **Important** tasks in your list, the ones labeled B. These too should be numbered from most important to least important using B-1, B-2, B-3 and so forth.

If you get these done and you have some remaining time, you can turn to something on the limited value list. However, I would challenge you to try to keep limited value stuff out of your life entirely, and off your to-do list. Why in the world would you want to spend time on something that has limited value when there are so many **URGENT,** *Vital* **and Important** things to accomplish? I realize the concept of keeping limited value items out of your life may seem daunting. However, I want to encourage you to try it, because the results you experience will be nothing short of liberating.

People often get stuck in a rut of doing the same activities over and over again without ever taking the time
to ask themselves why. Do they even enjoy bowling, let
alone the company of their bowling team members and
the league they've participated in every Wednesday night
for the past 17 years? If you love bowling, then keep on
bowling, but if you *don't* really enjoy it, call a time-out
and *unschedule* this activity.

The same goes for any old habit that doesn't really
nourish you or help you fulfill your goals. ***Get out of the
rut and back on the expressway.***

If you look at the **Monthly Planner** on pages 100-101
for Thursday, May 18, you will see that the list has been
prioritized using the coding explained above. Each item
has an *, an **A**, or a **B** next to it. (I did not put any C's
in this example, since it would have been a little hard to
read.) I list them here so you can see what order I decided
to do them in, as opposed to the order they were listed
in. As you can see, the first item I worked on that day was
the last item in the list of personal things to do. After I
complete the five **URGENT** items (*1-5), I began working
on A-1 of the Vital list, and the Important list of the B's.

Examples:

*-2: Birthday wish to Ralph.

B-3: Schedule meeting on productivity plan.

B-6: Write *The Main Street Diary* for June.

B-5: Schedule visits to see concierge lounges.

B-4: Give Rosemary restaurant feedback.

*-4: Thank you note to Jim.

A-1: Fix check-in at Hotel X.

*-3: Fix Bob.

B-1: Schedule appointment with financial advisor.

B-7: Open retirement savings account.

B-2: Schedule annual eye exam.

*-5: Schedule trip to *Magic Kingdom*® with kids.

B-8: Write letter to Mom.

*-1: Book ticket for vacation in September.

When I did my **planning time** that morning, I found many things to work on. Some were there when I opened my Day-Timer® to the 18th. I had put them there over the previous days or weeks, since my goal was to try to get them done on that day.

Always put things in your "To Be Done Today" list on a day that you think you'll have the best opportunity to get it done, taking into account your other tasks for the day. You want to try to balance your calendar and your "To Be Done Today" list, if you are in meetings all day you won't have much discretionary time to get to the *"To Be Done Today"* list. When I went through my mail on May 18, I added a few more items. Then I looked back at the day before, the 17th, and moved a couple of things forward that I had not been able to get done. I put one of those items on today's list, and moved another one to Friday, the 19th.

When I got to the *thinking* part of my **planning time**, I added "Fix check-in at Hotel X," because I saw a need there when I reviewed the customer satisfaction scores the day before. I also added "Fix Bob." Bob was one of my direct reports, and I decided that he needed some feedback on his recent poor performance, attitude and tardiness. I also added "Schedule appointment with financial advisor" and "Open retirement savings account" after reading an article in the Sunday paper that triggered my thinking on this subject.

This, by the way, is why it is so important to make time to read newspapers and magazines, and to find great websites to educate yourself on subjects relevant to your life and your interests. Having a broad base of knowledge and information can help a great deal when you have to make a calculated decision. Many times I have found a new way of thinking because of something I read! Reading good publications and viewing sources of online education like Thrive15.com will trigger ideas for you to work on.

After my list was complete for May 18, I put a priority on each item. Then I was ready to go. **I HAD A PLAN!**

A Day in the Life

My first appointment was at 8 a.m., with Erin and Karl. Referring to my notes in the "*Diary*" section reminded me of the things I wanted to discuss with them. The "*Diary*" section is the perfect place to create an agenda before a meeting. Erin and Karl left at 9 a.m. Since my next appointment was not until 10 a.m., I had an hour of discretionary time to do whatever I wanted to do.

The great thing about having a plan is that you don't waste your discretionary time. You go right to your plan and start chipping away at it. The first thing I wanted to do if I had any discretionary time that day was "Book my ticket for vacation in September." That item had *-1 (UR-GENT 1) next to it, indicating that I thought that it was the most **URGENT** thing on my list that day for one reason or another. Maybe it was the last day of a special price offer. After I took care of that, I recorded the trip in my **Advance Planner**, complete with flight numbers and departure and arrival times. That way, at any time, I could answer my family or colleagues if they asked when I would be away, what time I was leaving and exactly when I would be back. In my **Advance Planner**, this would be at my fingertips no matter where I am.

The next thing I worked on was *-2, then *-3, then *-4, and finally *-5. All of that was easy to accomplish in thirty minutes. Before I started on the next item, A-1, I was allowed to go the bathroom and get a glass of water, even though those items were not in the plan.

That was a joke! But if you are *really* disorganized, you may want to schedule events like those as well, until you get used to being organized.

So now it was 9:30 a.m., and I had to travel to *Disney's Animal Kingdom*® Theme Park for my walk with Beth Stevens. I dropped what I was working on and walked to my car. On the way, I took out my cell phone and returned some calls, which were listed in my Phone Call list in my Day-Timer®.

By the time I got to *Animal Kingdom* I had finished all the calls on my list except the one to our horticulture expert, which I took care of later in the day. She had some good ideas she wanted to share about flowering plants, so we decided to meet in Celebration, Florida when I would be in that area the following week. So I was able to check off that call on my list and enter the appointment time on the appropriate day.

I took an hour-long walk with Beth Stevens and drove back to the office. It was now 11:30 a.m. My next appointment was with Al Weiss, my boss, at 12 noon. I had thirty minutes of discretionary time. I had already eaten a peanut butter and jelly sandwich on the way back from *Animal Kingdom*, as I used to keep one in my briefcase on days when my schedule was tight. Saving thirty minutes on lunch helped me be on time for all my scheduled appointments. I did that infrequently, by the way, not just because I like good food, but because eating in the cafeteria was a great use of time. It enabled me to check the quality of the food, cleanliness and service, and also to meet and talk with *Disney Cast Members.*

It is amazing how time adds up, and how much more you can squeeze out of a day if you want to. Since I had thirty minutes, I got right to work on a *Vital* item, "Fix check-in at Hotel X." This was a big problem, and I wanted it to go away, so I determined to stay focused on it until it was fixed. All I could do that day was schedule a meeting two weeks later to move ahead on that project, with the goal of dramatically improving check-in six months later.

I then sent an e-mail to the nine people I wanted on my team to help with the project, explaining the problem and telling them that our first meeting would be from 2 p.m. to 4 p.m. on June 6, adding that they should block out every Wednesday from 2 p.m. to 4 p.m. for the next six months to work on the issue. I said we are going to fix the check-in problem by December 15, and they should start learning everything they can to prepare for our first meeting. I also asked them to let me know if there were others whom they thought should be on the Fix Check-In team. I gave them the location of the first meeting, and said that I would be available to meet with them one-on-one to discuss my expectations and their responsibilities. After I pushed the send key, I was done with this for the day.

The next day, in my **planning time**, I recorded all the new upcoming meetings in my calendar. Over the next couple of weeks I scheduled time to see each of my new team members and made sure we had space reserved for all our meetings in the coming months. Last but not least, I made an entry to let my boss know that we had begun the process of fixing the check-in problem before he brought it up from his side. Over the course of my career and my 46-year marriage, I learned that it's always better to notify your boss or your spouse about an obvious problem, including what you intend to do about it, before they bring it to your attention first. Thanks to Priscilla, I am an expert in this area.

I then checked that item as **done** for May 18. On the day of the team's first meeting, we brainstormed ideas and solutions and filled up flip charts, assigning responsibilities and due dates to everyone. By December, the problem was fixed, as planned.

That is what **focus** does. At *Disney*, whenever we chose to **focus** on something and invested the necessary time and resources, it was accomplished. The same concept will work in your life as well, personally and professionally. Focus on what you want to make better, set aside time for it, involve others to assist you and bingo, it won't be long before the problem is fixed.

Continuing on May 18, by the time my noon meeting with Al (my boss) rolled around, I had already completed my **URGENT** matters and my *Vital* issues for the day. Plus, I'd made sure to have that peanut butter and jelly sandwich handy, so I could have a quick lunch before meeting with Al. I was never late to a meeting with Al. I repeat, **<u>I WAS NEVER LATE TO A MEETING WITH AL.</u>** Maybe in your line of work reputations don't matter, but at *Walt Disney World*® being late to a meeting with a supervisor was not acceptable.

During our meeting, Al said, *"By the way, what are you doing about the check-in problem at Resort X?"* Boy, did I have a good story to tell him! He sat back and thought to himself, *This guy has his act together, and I like that.* That is where you want to be, at least one step in front of your boss, if not more. In fact, asking your boss from time to time if there is anything he or she would like you to be working on is a good technique for getting the right things into your plan. It is much better for your career if you have a plan rather than stammering and stuttering when you are asked what you are doing regarding something *Vital* to your business. A side benefit to getting out in front on the *Vital* tasks is that, when you attend to them effectively, many **URGENT** issues never arrive. This can save you gobs of time putting out fires and losing sleep over them.

If you ever have trouble remembering why *Vital* items are more important than the **Important** items on your list, remember that your vital organs— heart, lungs, kidneys, liver, etc.—are a lot more important than your other body parts, such as fingers, toes and the like. You really want to take care of the vital ones because you cannot live without them.

It is the same way with *Vital* issues in your business and personal life. When you fix check-in, you don't have to deal with angry guests about it. You have lower turnover with your front desk staff because the place is organized, and guests aren't yelling at them. You have increased repeat business and word of mouth because you are providing great customer service.

Another thing that could be listed as *Vital* is your health. Soon you should put in your planner **Fix My**

Health. If you don't spend the time to stay healthy you will need to set aside a lot of time to recuperate after your bypass surgery.

At 12:30 p.m. on May 18 I got back in the car and drove to the doctor's office for my annual physical. In the long run, this is a huge time-saver. Finding problems early is a big deal, especially where your health is concerned. How many times have you heard someone say, "If we had just discovered it sooner, he would be alive today." When I schedule medical appointments, I always try to make them for 8 a.m., because the only appointment doctors are on time for is their first one. Plus, he or she is rested up and paying attention at that time of morning.

Whenever possible, I also do the same for my airline flights. The first flight of the day has the best chance of leaving on time, because the plane is at the airport, as the plane has been stationed there the night before. The later in the day you travel the greater the potential for long delays, and that can become a real time-wasting nightmare. Remember, "The early bird gets the worm and the late bird gets the dirt."

When I finished my physical exam, I told the doctor which medications and vitamins I take, and the information was readily at hand because I had recorded it in my Day-Timer® under the doctor's name. I got back to my office at 3:30 having picked up my voicemail messages and returned a few more phone calls on my hands-free phone on the way. (Please don't drive while holding a cell phone to your ear, even if it's legal in your state; it's a serious hazard.) I then had thirty minutes until my 4 p.m. with Mary to do her performance review. I was already prepared for that meeting, as I had planned it the day before. So I had two choices: I could go around and bother other busy people, or I could get to work on item **B-1** on my list, then **B-2**, **B-3** and maybe even **B-4** before 4 o'clock.

I finished with Mary 15 minutes early, giving me time to start planning the next day before I left for my 5:15 workout appointment with myself. That appointment is in my book *every day*! That year, I had a goal of working out 275 days. I had the same goal the previous year, but I only made 273 before I ran out of days. The year before that, I hit 274. That means I missed my goal by three days over two years. That is annoying to me, and I determined that it wouldn't happen again, at least not for the same reasons. And it didn't.

My workout ended at 6:15. I had to cut it a little short that day so I could get to the birthday party for my friend James in Winter Park. Priscilla had to meet me at the party because my schedule was tight. But I did get my workout in because that was, and still is, a priority in my life—and one way to get your priorities accomplished is to schedule them into your calendar. This is a big point:

Schedule the priorities in your life directly into your calendar.

I don't care what anyone tells you about his or her priorities. The proof is in the pudding, and the ingredients of the pudding are the items scheduled in his or her calendar. I can't emphasize this enough: *Schedule the priorities in your life.* That means *all* your priorities, both business and personal.

At 9 p.m. I got home from the birthday party. I looked over my calendar for the next day, May 19, and made some last-minute notes based on events that occurred on the 18th. One entry was a reminder to send a thank you note to James and Jane for a great birthday party dinner, and to tell them how much Priscilla and I enjoyed meeting their children, Dan and Mary. During dinner, I flipped over to Saturday in my Day-Timer® and wrote down the name of the red wine they served so I could buy a bottle for myself. That little Day-Timer® sure comes in handy when you least expect it.

I also added to my *"To Be Done Today"* list for the week:

· *Write postcards to servicemen and servicewomen in Iraq and Afghanistan.*

· *Meet with a contractor to have my air-conditioning units checked. They are twelve years old and about ready for replacement.*

· *Submit reimbursement forms for medical expenses.*

· *Schedule visits to companies in the Orlando area to get them interested in running a United Way campaign this year.*

· *Buy a birthday gift for Daniel.*

· *Work on organizational structure ideas for changes in the way we are organized.*

I went to bed after brushing my teeth and flossing (flossing is a great time-saver because it reduces the number of dental visits you have to make). The last thing I did was tell Priscilla I love her—another time-saver, especially if you mean it as much as I do. Before I knew it, it was 5:10 a.m. and time to rise and shine on May 19.

That morning, I made Priscilla's coffee and a peanut butter and jelly sandwich for me. Then I packed my workout clothes, showered and dressed, and headed off to Starbucks. I arrived there at 5:50 a.m., settled in with a bowl of oatmeal with fruit and nuts and no sugar, my tall Pike and the *N.Y. Times* or *Wall Street Journal*. By 6:00 I was out the door. I arrived at my office at 6:15, only 65 minutes after I woke up. One big time-saver (and life-saver) I have come to appreciate over the years is to live close to work, even if you have to downsize. Another is to arrange your schedule to avoid traffic whenever possible.

It was 6:15 a.m. when I settled at my desk: **planning time** again, just like every other day. That is my routine. On that morning, I had to move **B-6**, **B-7** and **B-8** to another day of week, when I would have the best likelihood of getting them done. An item I did not get done yesterday ended up with a much higher **B** rating. This is the way priorities work. Sometimes a task elevates from *Vital* to **URGENT**.

Think of the life of a student. When he or she is given an assignment to do a term paper six weeks before it is due, it is an **Important** project. And if the student procrastinates, and the paper is suddenly due in three days, or one, it becomes an **URGENT** project.

Many things in our lives become **URGENT** because we are disorganized and we don't have a system for staying on top of our responsibilities. I have seen many brilliant people fail to live up to their potential because they weren't organized. No one cares how smart you are if you can't get anything done. As someone once said, "The only good ideas are the ones that get accomplished."

When you accomplish the items on your list, make it official by noting it in your planner. As you work through the day, use the following symbols to record your work in each category:

√   = **Completed**
/   = **Started but not completed**
( ) = **See or refer to**
→ = **Moved forward to another date**

Here are some additional thoughts on what we discussed:

We often don't get to the Vital items because we are so busy putting out the fires of the URGENT. And many of the URGENT items were created because we didn't get to them when they were only Vital. It's a vicious cycle, and you must discipline yourself to get out of it, or else you will spend your life being busy but not making a difference. At Walt Disney World® the cycle of procrastination, followed by extreme busyness to compensate for lack of planning, organization and action, was simply not tolerated. Sadly, however, I see that pattern at work in many organizations, where that kind of behavior is the norm. If you find yourself caught in a cycle of being perpetually busy but behind, you must decide right now that you are going to break free and begin forming new habits based on pro-activity and organization. You can do it.

If everyone in an organization did just one Vital thing a year, they would have to bring in large trucks to haul away the profits. And if you do one Vital thing a year in your personal life, you will be amazed at how much better and stress-free your life will be.

I try to think up a few **Vital** things every year in areas where I can get a big payback, or where I think can make a difference. I write those things in my Day-Timer®, which acts like an idea incubator. It's just a matter of time before that intention becomes a living thing. This is how we accomplish the things we'll be most proud of.

Writing down **Vital** tasks each year has become almost a game to me. If ever I have trouble thinking of one, I'm sure Priscilla would have one for me, and that would be just fine. In regards to priorities, my wife is at the top. I don't see her much during the week, so I make sure to spend every weekend with her as well as the other members of my family. They are a much higher priority than playing golf or other activities when we're not together. I am sure you can figure out why this is a good time management/life management practice. If you want to play golf all day on the weekends, my philosophy would be to make sure that you schedule something special for you and your loved one sometime during the week. Unless everyone important to you is happy, you don't and won't have a balanced life.

To sum up the message of this chapter:

Write things down
Plan your day and life, and
Schedule the priorities in your life,

You will be amazed, because you will be able to:

Do what has to be done,
when it has to be done,
in the way it should be done,
whether you like it or not!

In my career, I have been responsible for managing four people and I've been responsible for managing over 40,000 people, and I can tell you that until you learn to write things down, plan your day and schedule the priorities in your life, you will struggle in the areas of both time and life management.

The good news is that I've seen countless people learn to implement these new skills, and I've watched them begin to thrive as they become exponentially better at managing their lives. You can do it too. It's not overly complicated; it just requires self-discipline. Get started today, not someday.

That's it! Next, we will discuss how not to procrastinate, as well as many other subjects that relate to time management/life management. Some of it will surprise you! (See the Time Management Calendar on the next page.)

18

THURSDAY
MAY 18

APPOINTMENTS & SCHEDULED EVENTS

NAME • PLACE • SUBJECT

A.M.
6:15 - 8:00 OFFICE PLANNING TIME
8:00 - WEEKLY UPDATE WITH ERIN & KARL (5/18)

10:00 - WALK DAK WITH BETH STEVENS

NOON
P.M.
11:30 - AL UPDATE (5/18 DIARY)

1:00 - 3:00 ANNUAL PHYSICAL (B)
4-5 PDP REVIEW WITH MARY
5:15 WORKOUT

NTE
7:30 BIRTHDAY DINNER FOR JAMES (5/18 DIARY)

✓ TO BE DONE TODAY (ACTION LIST)

*2	BIRTHDAY NOTE TO RALPH - GRACE
B3	SCHED. MEETING ON PRODUCTIVITY PLAN
B6	WRITE MAIN STREET DIARY FOR JUNE
B5	SCHED VISIT TO CONCIERGE LOUNGES
B4	GIVE ROSEMARY RESTAURANT FEEDBACK (5/17)
*4	THANK YOU NOTE TO JIM
A1	FIX CHECK-IN
*3	FIX BOB

B1	SCHED APPT WITH FINANCIAL ADVISOR
B7	OPEN RETIREMENT SAVINGS ACCT
B2	SCHED YEARLY EYE EXAM
*5	SCHED VISIT TO M.K. WITH CHILDREN
B8	LETTER TO MOTHER
*1	BOOK AIR TICKETS FOR VACATION IN SEPT

EXPENSE & REIMBURSEMENT RECORD:

PHONE CALLS	Amount
CARL - 407-325-6543	
ELIZ JOHNSON 202-464-3251 (5/20	GUEST
BILL ROGERS 321-424-1564	CAST
AL - 3464	
FRANK MCMILLAN 407-322-4651	LAWYER.
GRACE - 251-625-8888	THANKS
PRISCILLA - 407-876-3072	

Monthly Planner with Daily Tasks Prioritized

DIARY AND WORK RECORD

HRS.	NAME OR PROJECT	DESCRIPTION	TIME

8 0800

7:30PM   DINNER JAMES HOUSE
I-4 TO LEE RD - TAKE RIGHT
GO 1.4 MILES TO OAK STREET - RIGHT
2 BLOCKS ON LEFT 546 OAK ST.
   407-414-3217   WIFE: JUDY
                    KIDS: DAN/MARY

9 0900

10 1000

8:00 ERIN / KARL UPDATE
 - REVIEW CONTINGENCY PLAN
 - DISCUSS ORGAN STRUCTURE
 - THANK THEM

11 1100

11:30   AL WEISS UPDATE
 - ORGAN STRUCTURE
 - OVERTIME
 - CONCERNS / ADVICE

12 1200

* PRISCILLA/GROCERY STORE/PICK UP ON WAY HOME
* MILK, BREAD, NY TIMES, STRAWBERRIES, GRAPES

1 1300

ELIZ. JOHNSON - LEE TO CALL GUEST
 - HAD POOR EXPERIENCE AT CHECK-IN
 - MARY RUDE
 - ROOM 6PM
 - CALL BACK BY 12N FRIDAY 5/19

2 1400

3 1500

4 1600

5 1700

"A year from now you will wish you started today."

KAREN LAMB

CHAPTER 5

Mom's Advice on Procrastination

...As In, Clean Up Your Room!

When I was young, my mother would often use a certain big word when she spoke to my brother and me. I remember her saying things like, "Would you stop procrastinating and get your room cleaned up?" or "Stop procrastinating and do your homework," or "Are you procrastinating again? I need that grass mowed." I knew the definition of *procrastination* all right, but I did not really understand it. I never focused on what the word meant to me personally until I was much older.

I remember telling my mom that I was *not* procrastinating. I said things like, "I plan to do it later," or "I forgot. I'll get right to it," or "I didn't have time." You know, all the basic excuses that everyone uses. I think I believed back then that procrastination was a character flaw, and there wasn't much anyone could do about it.

Well, after I took that Time Management class back in 1980 I knew better! I realized that in business, procrastination is a career killer and an ambition destroyer. I learned that being thought of as a procrastinator by your leaders or peers is perhaps the worst thing that could happen if you are trying to move up the career ladder. Procrastinator may be the worst thing you can be called in business other than "crook" or "thief." Henceforth, I started doing a number of things obsessively to build a reputation as the opposite of a procrastinator. I wanted to be seen as a proactive, seize-the-day person by both my peers and those in leadership positions above me.

Here's what I did, and I strongly urge you to do the same:

1) Schedule the priorities in your life, write them into your calendar, and keep those appointments.

2) Make a list of "to do's" every day during planning time, and put a priority on each item.

3) Think about your long-term goals every day as you do your planning time, and get started on them now so they come true down the road.

4) Keep the Vital tasks you are working on right in front of you on your desk to remind you often to get them done no matter what.

5) Break down really big projects into smaller pieces to get them done one step at a time—and call upon experts to help you.

6) Leave time in your calendar for interruptions and for things that come up at the last minute. Don't overbook your calendar.

7) Do the things you dislike first every day, so you don't spend the rest of the day thinking about them.

8) Develop and follow an administrative system that is simple and enables you to quickly put your hands on documents, information, phone numbers and addresses.

9) Know how to use technology to save time and make you more effective. Most people are not getting the total value out of their technological devices.

10) Commit to a deadline for your work, and also gain agreement on deadlines when you delegate to others or receive an assignment from your boss, spouse or partner. "June 5 at 5 p.m." is a deadline. "ASAP" and "When I get a chance" are not deadlines.

11) Select the best time of day to get work done for you. For me and for most business leaders that ideal time is in the morning—in my case, 6:15 am in the morning.

12) Learn to start projects as quickly as possible, so you have ample time to work and rework them. The earlier you begin, the better the outcome usually is.

13) And the big one: Learn to delegate properly and to trust others. Find experts to assist you in areas you are not strong in.

Rooting Out Timewasters

There are certainly a lot of timewasters in our lives these days. I recommend that you devote some of your planning time in the morning to thinking about the following:

Ask Yourself These Questions:

What wastes your time?

What can you do to eliminate these timewasters?

How can you use that time for things that are more productive and have higher value for business/personal use?

Which timewasters do you impose on yourself, and which are imposed on you by others?

Some great examples of self-imposed timewasters are:

1) *Sleeping in and not taking the time for planning before you start your day. Throughout my career I have noticed that nearly all of the most successful people on the planet are early risers.*

2) *Lack of self-discipline, which relates to number one above.*

3) *Taking on too much. You must learn when to say yes and when to say no.*

4) *Not delegating work, or not delegating properly, with clear directions and deadlines.*

5) *Missing the main message or teaching because you were not paying attention or not listening well. Being preoccupied is one of life's big timewasters, because you are physically present but not really present with your attention. Priscilla has often said to me, "Lee, are you listening to me?" I have had to plead guilty many times.*

6) *Not being realistic about how long something will take. Start early enough so that, even if you misjudge the duration, you will still have time to do quality work.*

7) Not anticipating all the complications that can arise, and therefore not planning for them or, better yet, making sure they don't happen at all.

8) Living too far from work.

9) Tolerating and effectively celebrating chronically late team members.

Great examples of timewasters imposed on us by others include:

1) Lack of a policy or operating guidelines.

2) Poorly run meetings that drag on too long.

3) Lack of authority.

4) Lack of feedback on performance.

5) Unclear job description.

6) Poor communication from others.

7) Waiting for decisions from others.

8) Problems not well-defined.

9) Being understaffed.

10) Being overstaffed.

11) Shifting priorities.

Take the time to list five to ten ways in which you currently waste time. What can you do about them if you focus on the problem? Once you figure that out, *focus on it and do it*! And for crying out loud, **QUIT PROCRAS-TINATING!** We already agreed that the only person who has half a chance of controlling the events in your life is you!

An example of something that I saw many people procrastinate on while I was at *Disney* was their Project Tomorrowland training. This is the kind of thing that was easy to put off unless Cast Members proactively scheduled the time to do it and got started early so they could take breaks along the way. About 92 percent of our team completed their training on time, but I bet there were a lot of last-minute **URGENTS** on their lists before they got it done. As for those who did not make it to the finish line, eight percent may sound like a small number to you, but that adds up to 800 to 1,000 people, and they had months to get it done.

Taxes are another thing most people procrastinate about. On January 1, "Do the taxes" is an **Important** item. But on April 14, it is **URGENT!** So is Christmas shopping on December 24.

As a general rule, without looking too deep into their individual files, I can tell you that 95 percent of the people who did not finish that Project Tomorrowland training on time have not gone far within the organization and are unlikely to be considered for leadership positions in the future. That's because they acquired a reputation as an excuse-making procrastinator. In business, and life in general, we earn our reputations based upon what we do, not on what we intend to do. You can choose to be known as dependable and proactive or as an unreliable procrastinator.

Getting Better and Better

Okay, now that we have learned about the true meaning of procrastination and a little more about how to eliminate timewasters in our lives, let's go on to how you can grow and become better and better as a person, leader, parent, spouse, companion, community leader and every other part of your life you would like to focus on.

If you don't really know what is important, you will find it difficult to focus on what you need to do to reach your goals. So take some time to make a list of the things you value most. I will give you the list that I made thirty-five years ago as an example of what I mean.

Back then I listed these items:

1) Get healthy and stay healthy.
2) Gain respect from others and give respect to others.
3) Be a better leader.
4) Have high personal performance.
5) Have strong family relationships.
6) Become financially secure.

That was my list.

Here are some things I've heard others say they valued most:

1) Become more humble (Respect all people and show it).
2) Become more authentic (Tell the truth and admit mistakes).
3) Become better informed (Read more).
4) Improve my self-confidence and self-esteem.
5) Be more organized. (Take a time management course).
6) Gain trust from people (Take time to get to know them and help them).
7) Become a better public speaker (You cannot do this the night before a speech).

Once you take the time to figure out what you would like to improve or achieve, you can use your day planner and the other resources available to help you get to work on those things. Some aspects of life will improve if you simply keep them in the forefront of your mind, while others will require some hard work or outside help. But identifying them is half the battle.

One of the greatest reasons people don't improve is because they are not honest with themselves. They lack the ability to see their own faults and weaknesses. No education or training is complete without self-reflection. As the leader of nearly 40,000 employees I had to become very aware of my own faults so I could begin improving immediately.

You have to get better, faster!

Look at your last employee satisfaction survey, or whatever the equivalent is in your company. And if you don't already do so, I strongly suggest that you implement such a survey annually, to find out what your team members are thinking about and what they want to see improved. If you're a leader, you'll especially want to know what concerns your employees have about your leadership. Read between the lines of their comments and messages. Pay close attention to what your family and friends say with their comments, body language and facial expressions. The problems are there if you look for them.

Once those problem areas are identified, you can fix them. There is very little that most people can't do if they really put their minds to it, and if they have a vision of what the future can look like once they address the issues brought to their attention. Priscilla has given me feedback on several shortcomings, like my driving, my need to say "I'm sorry" with sincerity and the importance of becoming a better listener. I think she agrees that I've done a pretty good job of improving on those traits, and I'm grateful for her indispensable help in making me a better person. She continues to show me things and I hope she is equally successful in the future.

Many individuals don't attempt to have a great life. Why? Because they have a pretty good life, and they settle for that. But why be satisfied with average, when great is achievable? Think about how different *Walt Disney World*® would be—or if it would exist at all—if Walt *Disney* had been content with mediocrity. Would we have *Snow White, Bambi, Frozen* or *The Lion King* if the leaders of *Disney* were content with just being average?

We are all guilty of living in our comfort zones, and we often resist taking chances or trying new things because we have that basic fear of failure. Highly successful people are often afraid too, but here's the difference–they take calculated risks and go for it anyway. Without taking risks you can't be great. I did not have an average career. I did not have a good career. I had a *great* career, because I took a lot of risks along the way.

Setting Goals

Setting goals can be just plain uncomfortable at times, but if you don't set goals you will not know if or when you get there. A goal can be an inspiring thing, and usually, when you tell others what your goal is, they will help you get there!

One of the most important steps in accomplishing your goals is to *write them down*. This single step makes a huge difference. When you write it down, it becomes much clearer.

The act of writing turns an intangible thought into something concrete, and we need that if we are to turn what we imagine into reality.

Here are some tips about goal-setting:

- *Be specific about what your goal is.*

- *Express the goal in a way that makes it possible to measure results. If it is not measurable, it is not really a goal.*

- *Make sure the goal is something you really want, as opposed to something that someone else wants for you. My mother wanted me to be a dentist. That was not my goal, and I could not get as excited about it as she was.*

Here are some examples of goals:

1) *Lose 30 pounds by December 1.*
2) *Work out 90 minutes a day, 5 days a week, starting on May 1.*
3) *Reduce my expenses by 10% by September 30.*
4) *Spend four hours a month doing something together with each of my children.*
5) *Take my wife out to dinner once a month.*
6) *Get my annual physical by June 15.*

You get the idea.

And setting goals applies to all aspects of life. You can set goals for your:

- *Professional development and career*
- *Financial planning for your future*
- *Areas of health, including exercise, diet, weight and sleep*
- *Areas of cultural and intellectual improvement*
- *Learning more about using technology*

And so on.

Once you set your goals, do not hesitate to ask for help in achieving them. And make sure you ask yourself the one big question that most people fail to think about: *Am I prepared to pay the price to achieve this goal?* Is your goal to run a marathon? Well, you'd better be prepared to pay the price of training. My friend Dieter Hannig's goal is to climb Mount Everest. Well, there is a huge price to pay physically and financially to achieve that, and Dieter knows it. What about the goal of becoming a leader? Have you thought about the price that leaders pay with their time? And the stress level and pressure of making difficult decisions day in and day out? Always take into account a realistic appraisal of the cost-to-benefit ratio that comes into play when you set a goal.

You can use my first two books, *Creating Magic* and *The Customer Rules,* to get ideas about goals to focus on, and as a way to stimulate your thinking. When you review those books, remember that they can be applied to your business life or your personal life, but preferably both. Watch for my two forthcoming books: *Career Development Magic–How to Stay on Track to Achieve a Stellar Career* will teach you how to keep your career on track and *Storytelling Magic–Setting Direction for Your Organization Through Story Telling,* which is about exactly what the title says.

Okay, I have to go now. I have to get to the meeting in my day planner. Have a great day contemplating the goals you hope to accomplish!

"The ability to concentrate and to use your time well is everything if you want to succeed in business or almost anywhere else for that matter."

LEE IACOCCA

CHAPTER 6

Priscilla's Advice on Preoccupation
...As In, Pay Attention!

Now we will move into some areas that you might not have thought of in relation to managing your time better. Preoccupation is one of the biggest timewasters, and it applies to every part of our lives. "Preoccupation" is sometimes defined as not paying attention, and when you are not paying attention to the pertinent happenings around you, you miss things that you should be taking care of. When you are not paying attention because you are thinking of something else, time is wasted, because someone will have to explain things to you a second time or, worse, you will do the wrong thing because you were not listening carefully.

For a great example, try talking to someone who is watching television—especially a child. Try telling small children to clean up their rooms, or to do *anything* for that matter, while they are watching TV.

It is highly unlikely they will even hear your instructions. Chances are they will not hear a single word you say. They won't even look at you. At least with children, you know they are not listening. Adults know how to fake it.

Husbands are notorious for hearing their wives talk, but without taking their eyes off the television long enough to actually hear what they are being told. At least that's what Priscilla tells me! I try to tell her that it's not our fault; it's just our programming. She has not bought that excuse yet, but it is the only explanation that makes any sense to me. So, all you guys out there: when you hear the words, "are you listening to me?" it's not a question, it's a statement and a warning. Simply saying "Yes, dear" does not cut it. I strongly suggest turning off the TV for a minute so there is no breakdown in communication.

Being preoccupied invariably leads to misunderstandings. Have you ever been in a meeting when someone asks, "What do you think about this?" and you are forced to say, with an embarrassed look on your face, "What was that? I didn't hear you. Can you repeat that?" Of course, you did not hear the question because you were not paying attention. You were preoccupied. You were thinking about your next meeting or about lying on a beach somewhere.

Sometimes the consequences are a lot worse, like if you're rear-ended by a car because the driver behind you was preoccupied—with a cell phone, most likely—instead of paying attention to driving safely.

People today are more preoccupied than ever. At meetings, they even pay more attention to their smartphones and tablets than to what is being said. Paying attention to others is an important responsibility at work, no matter what level of responsibility you have. If you're a leader, get out from behind your desk and listen to your people. Remember that what they say and what they are really trying to tell you are usually two different things.

In every aspect of your life, it is your responsibility to focus sharply so you are able to make the right decisions. Pay attention to that special person in your life, to your children, to your leader at work, to your direct reports, to your friends, relatives and everyone else. They will appreciate it, and you will be much more effective and efficient. Additionally, people will take notice and your reputation will be enhanced.

Here are some ways to get out of the bad habit of being preoccupied:

- *Take notes when someone is telling you something, so you stay engaged.*

· *Get into a position where you can focus exclusively on the person and hear what he or she is saying. I always found it best to sit with the people I was meeting with, rather than stay behind my desk across from them. When you have no physical barriers between you and the other person, you have a much better chance of clear, focused communication.*

· *Never try to sneak in reading an e-mail or a text, or a phone call while someone is trying to explain something to you.*

· *In meetings, sit next to the boss or in the front row. This will help you stay focused and not drop off into dreamland.*

· *Focus on one thing at a time if you want to be a good communicator, save time and do great work.*

· *Stay in good physical condition by eating properly, exercising and getting the right amount of sleep—and in warm climates like Florida, by drinking enough water. When you are physically fit, you feel good, and when you feel good, you are able to pay attention without fading out due to lack of sleep or a poor diet. High energy is a time-saver. Being fit also helps you manage stress, and stress can erode your ability to pay attention. Of course, your Day-Timer® can help you by controlling your calendar for things like scheduling workouts, making sure you get enough sleep and recording what you eat so you can understand the effects of different foods on your body and mind. (I use my smartphone to look up the calories in food before I order it or eat it.)*

Time-Saving Meetings

· *One way to save time for you and others is to be very responsible when you run a meeting. Make sure that you schedule an appointment with yourself in your day planner the day before the meeting, so you can prepare for it to start on time, run efficiently and end on time, or early if possible. Few things make people as happy as getting out of a meeting early, except perhaps having the meeting canceled. In the business world, meetings have a reputation as a waste of time. You can buck the trend by having such great meetings that people actually look forward to them and consider them a great use of time.*

· *Always use an agenda to run a meeting. Otherwise, it will wander all over the place and the level of efficiency will plummet. Try to run your meetings in a way that actually helps people do their jobs better.*

· *There are two kinds of meetings, and they should be held separately. The purpose of one is to give out information, and the purpose of the other is to solve problems. You don't want to try to solve a specific problem in a meeting designed to give out information, because you will have people in the room who have nothing to do with the problem. You will be wasting their time, and they'll wonder why they are there?" Schedule meetings to address specific problems separately, and invite only those people whom you need to solve the problem.*

· *Here's another time-saving tip: conclude meetings and phone calls quickly. Learn how to get right to the point. When a meeting seems to be slowing down, summarize your understanding of everyone's responsibilities and ask the participants if there is anything else you need to know. When they say "No," stand up to signal that the meeting is over. Wrapping up meetings and phone calls efficiently has saved me thousands of hours during my career.*

· *After the meeting, make sure to write down what you agreed to do and the new responsibilities you may have taken on in the "Diary" section of your Day-Timer®. Follow up the next day during planning time.*

• *Here's another thing to consider: Is the meeting necessary in the first place. Always ask people why they want to meet with you. You may be the wrong person for them to talk to. And if you are the right person, it might be more efficient to address their concerns by phone and/or e-mail. Face-to-face meetings are very important, but they are not always necessary. Don't meet with people just because they ask to meet with you.*

More Time-Saving Tips

Here are some other ways to save time:

• *Have everything you need at your fingertips. If you don't have the supplies, materials and resources you need to do your work immediately handy you will waste time running around looking for them. Inventory the important items from time to time to make sure they're within reach. Searching for something as simple as a pair of scissors or a phone number can waste a lot of your time.*

• *Involve others who are experts to help you make decisions. Often, that means people in frontline positions. Who knows more about check-in at a resort than the desk employee who checks in hundreds of guests a week? That's who I turned to when I discov-*

ered a check-in problem at one of the hotels I ran. So ask yourself from time to time:

- *What am I doing now that doesn't need to be done by me or my direct reports?*

- *What am I doing that someone else could be trained to do?*

- *What am I doing that I would be willing to pay someone else to do, to free up time to do what is more important?*

- *Create an environment where people feel safe to say what is on their minds, and where everyone is excited about their work because they are respected, listened to and really valued. If you respect, appreciate and value everyone, you will save more time than you can ever calculate. Your teams will do better work, and many problems will never surface in the first place. When people trust you, and you are humble, sincere, enthusiastic, cooperative and caring, the time you save cannot be measured by a clock. You may think it's a waste of time to listen to frontline employees, but I assure you it's exactly the opposite. You can't imagine how much time I saved during my career at Disney because I took the time to listen.*

· *Think of yourself as an environmentalist. Find ways to make your working environment better by your leadership, your attitude, your behavior and your presence. Supply your people with a wonderful environment where they can perform up to their capabilities—and even exceed them. Create an environment and a culture in which everyone matters, and they know they matter, and you will go from good to great and great to greater.*

· *Acknowledge your team—and your family and friends—every day. Tell them how great they are by complimenting them and rewarding them, either with real physical stuff or kind, respectful, personal words. As they say, "People will not remember what you said, but they will always remember how you made them feel." It's also true that nobody cares how much you know until they know how much you care. Be careful about what you say and do, because you are being watched and judged by everyone around you.*

Finally, remember that you are the one with the most control over how your life turns out.

It's Your Time, and It's Your Life!

"Once you have mastered time, you will understand how true it is that most people overestimate what they can accomplish in a year–and underestimate what they can achieve in a decade."

LOUIS E. BOONE

CHAPTER 7

Final Thoughts

...As In, When Are You Going to Get Started?

I hope you have picked up some good ideas and techniques for managing your career and all other parts of your life. I can tell you with all sincerity that the biggest goals and dreams of Walt Disney, Conrad Hilton or Bill Marriott would not have come to pass if it were not for the extreme focus that they and their leadership teams placed on time management. I can also tell you that if you hold yourself accountable to becoming the most efficient and effective time/life manager you can be, nearly anything is possible.

Now I am going to share with you my final thoughts and give you some ideas on how to get started. Once you learn something new that you believe in and want to implement, you have to get started immediately so you can start adopting and adapting to new skills and habits.

So, right away, you want to order a Day-Timer® or some kind of planner if you don't already have one, or use your smartphone to perform the same tasks just as well. I told you earlier that I use the Two-Page-Per-Day Original, which is Product #98010. Go to <u>www.daytimer.</u> <u>com</u> and they'll send it right off to you so you can get started. A good alternative is the Franklin Planner (www. franklinplanner.com). The company also offers time management seminars in various cities.

The Day-Timer® I use comes with a vinyl cover. Later on, if you like the system as much as I do, you might want to order a leather cover. They are expensive, but maybe someone will give you one for your birthday if you leave enough hints around.

I can't emphasize this enough: *you simply must use a planner if you really want to manage your time successfully.* A planner, or your smartphone if that works better for you, can be used for so many things. Some of them we've discussed, but I have put examples below:

    · *Remembering special events, birthdays, anniversaries, etc.*

    · *Remembering to give someone some positive feedback and recognition.*

- *Remembering to reward someone.*

- *Remembering to acknowledge someone for something he or she did for you, or to simply say thank you.*

- *Improving your communication with people.*

- *Scheduling all events in your life–ALL of them!*

The list is endless.

I also recommend that you get a Tri-Point pen that has red ink, black ink, pencil lead and an eraser. I call this pen my magic wand. When I pull it out and write things down in my planner, the magic begins to happen. It is remarkably efficient as you work through your day, since there are times when you need a pencil, like when you record appointments and schedule events that might change and need to be erased. I use the red ink to check things off as I accomplish them, and the black or blue ink to write notes and letters, sign documents, etc.

The Cross Pen Company sells this pen, and you can find it, along with refills, at places like Office Depot. I assure you that seeing your planner full of red check marks is one of the best feelings in the world.

More Time-Saving Tips

Using a planner will change your life. But there are many other ways to more effectively manage your time.

Here are some I've learned along the way:

· *Improve your communication skills, so when you give instructions to people or delegate responsibilities to them, you are crystal clear. To ensure clarity, have them repeat back to you what they heard.*

· *Listen more carefully and take notes to help you understand what you are hearing.*

· *Ask more questions to make sure you understand what you are hearing, and to clear up what you don't understand. Take 100 percent responsibility for your communication with others.*

· *Make sure to take five to thirty minutes to plan every day. This is a key strategy. Having personally witnessed some of the most successful leaders at the world's most successful companies, I believe that it is almost impossible to be successful without taking the time to plan each day.*

· *Think every day about things you should be working on that won't pay off for months or years.*

· *Make sure you spend time focusing on vital tasks that will give the most return for your customers, employees, business results and personal life. These may not be easy, but you need to get started on them, and don't forget to ask for help if you run into physical or mental barriers.*

· *Identify the things you do that waste time and eliminate them.*

· *Learn to run meetings efficiently, using an agenda and starting and stopping on time.*

· *Record your personal goals in your day planner or phone to stay on top of them.*

· *When you delegate something, no matter how simple, trace its progress in your planner to make sure it gets done. This will improve your reputation for being organized and on top of things.*

· *If you make New Year's resolutions, use your planner to schedule and follow up on them, so you're sure to accomplish them. And remember, you don't have to wait until the new year to make resolutions and get started on something that will help make you, your loved ones or your organization better.*

· *When you make your list each morning, think about things your leader would want you to accomplish.*

· *Identify the things that will give a big payoff to your business or personal life if you get them done.*

· *Get started on tasks early, so you have enough time to take a break and still complete them on time.*

· *Think about which tasks would make you feel especially good when you get them done, and put them in your planner.*

· *Think about which tasks would make your boss or your family feel especially good when they're done, and put them in your planner.*

· *Look for items that need to get done today because of company operating guidelines, policy, legality, integrity or your personal values.*

· *Review this book from time to time to remind yourself of what you are not doing.*

No regrets

Nothing is sadder than someone growing old tormented by regret. I've heard it many times, "I wish I had spent more time with my son. I wish I had talked to my daughter about the birds and the bees when I first thought of it. I wish I had not smoked. I wish I had watched my diet and weight and exercised more. I wish I had gone back to school. I wish I had told her I loved her more often. I wish, I wish, I wish, I hope, I hope, I hope, I pray, I pray, I pray..." How many regrets do you want to have? How many regrets *will* you have if you don't plan and use your time effectively?

If you ever watched *The A-Team* on television back in the 80's, one thing they said in every episode was, "I love it when a plan comes together." At *Disney* and other hugely successful companies, they plan well and pay close attention to the details. If you pay attention to the details, you won't have regrets later on. The following are some tips:

Remember, there are just two kinds of decisions: *reversible and irreversible.* Reversible decisions can be implemented much faster than the irreversible ones. Make sure you know the difference before you make your decision.

Carefully review yesterday's page in your planner every morning, and make sure you leave nothing behind.

Think of the things you want to do and need to do. Then use your planner and all other resources at your disposal to make them happen. For instance, as I was writing this chapter I made a note to put my tax documents in order and mail them to my tax accountant on April 1st. I did it, and put it in the mail that morning. Had I not scheduled it in my planner, I probably would have forgotten to mail the documents. Because I planned for that detail, the task was done and taken care of! The IRS does not forgive you. They fine you!

Another example: I made a note to buy stuff for my grandchildren for their Easter baskets. Margot loved her Barbie Band-Aids, Tristan really loved his pacifiers and Julian was excited to get some puzzles. They expected to get candy, but these things were special. I also put IOUs in their plastic eggs. They love them, especially when one of the IOUs is for a trip to the Apple Store.

I also made a note to have my air-conditioner checked before the summer begins. There is no end to the things that you can put in your planner to follow up on.

Final Thoughts:

- *Don't just think about what you want to do and do not want to do. Think about your responsibilities in the different parts of your life.*

- *Think about what you must do now to ensure that you will not just prevail but thrive.*

Never underestimate what you personally can do for yourself and others. And remember, if you don't schedule it, it won't happen.

Get started today. Yes, today! Best wishes in managing your time and your life! I hope that all your dreams come true!

Finally, remember the words of Peter Pan from Walt Disney's *Peter Pan* Movie:

"The dreams you plan really can come true."

Lee Cockerell Resources

Great leaders look for the better way every day!!!!

Go to *www.LeeCockerell.com* for additional resources on leadership, management and service excellence, including my *Creating Magic – Leadership and Coaching on the Go* app, *Lessons in Leadership* Podcast and Blog and my books, *Creating Magic: 10 Common Sense Leadership Strategies from a Life at Disney, The Customer Rules: The 39 Essential Rules for Delivering Sensational Customer Service. Time Management Magic: How To Get More Done Every Day and Move from Surviving to Thriving,* and my new book *Creating Career Magic: How to Survive and Thrive the Ups and Downs* which will be published on September 30, 2016.

There is a wealth of information available to assist you in strengthening your leadership skills. Study and read about leadership and management every day. The more you put in your mind about these subjects, the more resources you will have to call on when you are faced with difficult issues to solve in your life.

To experience powerful, engaging and continual ongoing education from me, NBA Hall of Fame basketball player David Robinson and countless millionaires, everyday success stories and time management masters, visit: *www.Thrive15.com.*

When logging onto Thrive15.com, enter the promo code **MAGIC** to receive your 30-day trial to the most engaging online classroom ever created for business people. And remember, when you sign up, an armed services veteran gets a free membership.

Also visit my site: *www.TheSportsMindInstitute. com* to take online classes and learn from the most accomplished leaders in sports and business. Bulk discounts available.

About The Author... Lee Cockerell

Lee Cockerell is the former Executive Vice President of Operations for the *Walt Disney World®* Resort. As the Senior Operating Executive for ten years Lee led a team of 40,000 Cast Members and was responsible for the operations of 20 resort hotels, 4 theme parks, 2 water parks, a shopping & entertainment village and the ESPN sports and recreation complex in addition to the ancillary operations which supported the number one vacation destination in the world.

One of Lee's major and lasting legacies was the creation of *Disney Great Leader Strategies* which was used to train and develop the 7000 leaders at *Walt Disney World®*. Lee has held various executive positions in the hospitality and entertainment business with Hilton Hotels for 8 years and the Marriott Corporation for 17 years before joining *Disney* in 1990 to open the *Disneyland Paris* project.

Lee has served as Chairman of the Board of Heart of Florida United Way, the Board of Trustees for The Culinary Institute of America (CIA), the board of the Production and Operations Management Society and the board of Reptilia, a Canadian attractions and entertainment company. In 2005, Governor Bush appointed Lee to the Governor's Commission on Volunteerism and Public Service for the state of Florida where he served as Chairman of the Board.

He is now dedicating his time to public speaking, authoring a book on leadership, management and service excellence titled, *Creating Magic–10 Common Sense Leadership Strategies from a Life at Disney* which is now available in 13 languages and his previous book, *The Customer Rules–The 39 Essential Rules for Delivering Sensational Service.* Most recently, Lee has released his newest book, *Career Magic–How to Stay on Track to Achieve a Stellar Career.*

Lee also performs leadership and service excellence workshops and consulting for organizations around the world as well as for the *Disney Institute.*

Lee has received the following awards:

★ *Golden Chain Award for Outstanding leadership and business performance from the Multi-Unit Foodservice Operations Association (MUFSO).*

★ *Silver Plate Award for Outstanding Operator in the foodservice industry from the International Foodservice Manufacturers Association (IFMA).*

★ *Excellence In Production Operations Management and Leadership (POMS) from the Productions and Operations Management Society.*

★ *Grandfather of the year from his three grandchildren, Jullian, Margot and Tristan.*

Lee and his wife Priscilla live in Orlando, Florida.

Please contact Lee Cockerell at Lee@LeeCockerell.com for keynote addresses, workshops, consulting, executive coaching, and seminars on leadership, management and world-class customer service. Phone: 407-908-2118.

Other Books by Lee Cockerell

Creating Magic

10 Common Sense Leadership Strategies From A Life At Disney - Based on the principles taught at the World Renowned Disney Institute.

Creating Magic shows all of us – from small business owners to managers at every level – how to inspire employees, delight customers and achieve extraordinary business results just like Lee did at *Disney World.*

Creating Magic by Lee Cockerell – 270 pages
Available in Hardback, Paperback, E-book and Audio Book

The Customer Rules

The 39 Essential Rules for Delivering Sensational Service

Lee shares indispensable rules for serving customers with consistency, efficiency, creativity, sincerity and distinction. Lee shows why the customer always rules and presents instructions for serving customers so well they'll never want to do business with anyone but YOU.

The Customer Rules by Lee Cockerell – 208 pages
Available in Hardback, Paperback, E-book and Audio Book

Career Magic

How to Stay on Track to Achieve a Stellar Career

A unique book full of priceless advice and insightful experience. Lee Cockerell chronicles how he went from being a college dropout, rose through the ranks at both *Hilton* and *Marriott*, and ultimately became the Executive Vice President of Operations for *Walt Disney World® Resorts.*

Career Magic by Lee Cockerell – 280 pages
Available in Hardback and E-book

Available at www.LeeCockerell.com, Online Retailers and Bookstores Nationwide